Getting Smarter Every Day

BOOK E

Grades 6–8

Created by
Dale Seymour

DALE SEYMOUR PUBLICATIONS®
Parsippany, New Jersey

Executive Editor: Catherine Anderson
Editorial Manager: John Nelson
Project Editor: Christine Freeman
Production/Manufacturing Director: Janet Yearian
Production/Manufacturing Manager: Karen Edmonds
Production/Manufacturing Coordinator: Joan Lee
Design Director: Phyllis Aycock
Design Manager: Jeff Kelly
Cover Design: Lynda Banks
Text Design: Nancy Carroll and Dale Seymour
Geometric Illustrations: Dale Seymour
Cartoon Illustrations: Bob Larsen
Page Composition: Alan Noyes

This book is published by Dale Seymour Publications®,
an imprint of Pearson Learning.

Dale Seymour Publications
299 Jefferson Road
Parsippany, NJ 07054-0480
Customer Service: 800-872-1100

Major League Baseball, World Series, American League,
and National League are registered trademarks of Major
League Baseball Enterprises, Inc.

Order number DS 21914
ISBN 0-7690-0111-4

This Book Is Printed
On Recycled Paper

1 2 3 4 5 6 7 8 9 10-ML-04 03 02 01 00 99

Contents

Puzzles, Challenges, and Activities by Concept

Helping Young People Get Smarter Every Day

Getting *Smarter Every Day* is a selection of activities, puzzles, ideas, information, and graphics to excite, enrich, challenge, instruct, amaze, and entertain students. This book aims to broaden student perspectives on what mathematics really is and its application in the real world.

Numeracy and *Getting Smarter Every Day*

Wouldn't it be nice if students could "play" with numbers the way they do with balls or musical instruments? Wouldn't it be nice if students had a good feeling for what mathematics really is? Wouldn't it be nice to provide students with mathematics instruction that contributes to *numeracy,* the ability to understand and apply mathematics in everyday life?

Students often see mathematics only as arithmetic, because that is all they have been shown. They see mathematics as a series of algorithms to memorize, then apply to numbers, with a single answer as a result. Mathematics may also seem a solitary subject, without teamwork and sharing. Relatively few students explore the mathematical subjects they encounter, seeing no room for creativity.

Four major instructional approaches break through those barriers to promote numeracy, and *Getting Smarter Every Day* materials encourage and support such approaches.

Discussion and interaction. *Getting Smarter Every Day* presents puzzles that students and teachers will want to talk about. Students learn from each other. An interesting problem may have many parts; so, students with different learning styles may all experience success contributing to a group solution. When mathematics materials offer students opportunities for brainstorming, for enlightened discussion, they can discover beauty and excitement in a subject they will want to explore even further.

Active exploration. Active participation and discovery help students see the concrete aspects of mathematics, setting the stage for later generalization and abstraction. *Getting Smarter Every Day* prompts students to look for mathematical patterns in both numbers and images. When students make such discoveries themselves, they remember the relevant concepts better. Students are more likely to want to explore mathematics when they feel they have an individual role in those discoveries. Mathematics has room for creativity, for multiple methods and approaches.

Visualization and estimation. Everyday applications of mathematics frequently involve visualization and estimation. Students who are visual learners but not strong in math gain greater understanding (and enthusiasm) for mathematics through the many visual-thinking puzzles and activities in *Getting Smarter Every Day* (identified in the activity-concept grid on pages iv and v). Such selections also help students who are not skilled visual learners improve visualization skills. Though *Getting Smarter Every Day* does not specifically focus on estimation, its content involves estimating in many mathematical settings, such as probability, patterns, measurement, and visual perception. Group discussion of specific worksheets can provide many opportunities for exploring the process and value of estimation.

Interrelating concepts. Working on nonroutine, multi-step problems triggers students to use and become comfortable with a holistic approach to finding mathematical solutions. Such an approach requires teachers frequently to tie topics together. Just as a jigsaw puzzle becomes easier as more pieces fit together, so the solution of problems become easier as students connect mathematical ideas. Many materials in *Getting Smarter Every Day* involve multiple mathematical issues. The interplay of these issues is shown in the activity-concept grid on pages iv and v.

Overview of *Getting Smarter Every Day*

This is Book E in a series of six books (A through F) in the *Getting Smarter Every Day* series. This book is for students of varying skill levels in grades 6 through 8. Mathematical prerequisites for most activities are basic. (For activities suitable for students not working up to grade level or ability, also see Book D. For activities suitable for students working above 8th-grade level, also see Book F.)

Getting Smarter Every Day Book E contains approximately 100 worksheets. They are not intended for use page-by-page in numerical sequence. Rather, "pick and choose," selecting activities for a specific purpose. In general, the difficulty of activities increases from the front of the book to the back. The topics and concepts included often do not appear in regular classroom texts and, admittedly, are favorites of the author. The broad concepts included are:

- computation
- geometric relationships
- logic
- numeration
- part-whole relationships
- pre-algebra
- problem solving
- visual thinking

On pages iv and v, a grid identifies the specific worksheets in *Getting Smarter Every Day* that address each of these concepts. Teachers can use this grid in several ways. For instance, if students enjoy a specific topic or puzzle, the teacher can use the grid to locate similar activities for immediate follow-up that lets the class practice newly-discovered problem-solving techniques.

For even more activities on a topic, *Getting Smarter Every Day* also includes More Smart Books (pages 118 and 119), a list of specific books with related worksheets. This list is keyed to the specific worksheets in this book. Also look at Smart Math Web Sites, on page 120.

Worksheet completion time for the average student varies but generally ranges from 15 to 45 minutes. Perceived difficulty will vary considerably, as ability also ranges considerably in most mathematics classes in this grade range. For a more specific estimate of time requirement, and to assess appropriateness of a worksheet for a specific class, try an activity before assigning it.

Ways to Use This Book

This book is a resource whose pages teachers may use as blackline masters to reproduce worksheets for their own classroom or for specific students. Teachers may also use these pages to create overhead transparencies.

Warmups. *Getting Smarter Every Day* worksheet pages serve nicely as warmup handouts or overhead transparencies. The teacher may give the students five to ten minutes to work on an activity (while handling attendance and homework collection), then have a brief class discussion on questions, ambiguities, and strategies. If needed, the class may complete the worksheet during class time or as regular or optional homework.

Enrichment. In a typical class, student ability and interest spread is amazing. The teacher then faces quite a task to challenge each student. *Getting Smarter Every Day* worksheets serve well as "selected activities" for specific students.

Introduction to a new topic. If students have become accustomed to the style and pace of their mathematics textbook, they may expect the next chapter to feel just like the one preceding it, holding little excitement. As a surprise, teachers can grab student attention by using a relevant problem, puzzle, or activity from *Getting Smarter Every Day*. The challenge of a puzzle often has more motivational appeal than, "Now, turn to page..."

Extension or review of a concept. Teachers may use *Getting Smarter Every Day* worksheets to give students extra practice or review of a textbook topic. The worksheets may also provide an application of or connection with a recently-studied topic. A great way to extend a topic is to have students make a problem or a puzzle of their own. Several puzzle formats in this book lend themselves to that kind of extension. Often, students really understand a concept for the first time when they create their own problem.

Bulletin boards. Several pages in *Getting Smarter Every Day* present a graphic image without an activity assignment. Photocopies (perhaps at an enlarged scale) of these images make intriguing bulletin board materials. You may also display copies of such images that students have colored, outlined, or otherwise modified to display a variety of patterns within such images.

Assessing Student Results in *Getting Smarter Every Day*

Though *Getting Smarter Every Day* emphasizes thinking and process, teachers (and students) often want to know the "right" answer to puzzles and challenges. Experience with these materials will show that sometimes, even in mathematics, there is more than one "right" answer.

Answers. Solutions are provided in Smart Answers, starting on page 111. For many of the problems in *Getting Smarter Every Day*, answers are not unique. Praise students who get different answers, if their answers are correct. Use such experiences to help students see that, in the real world, a problem often has more than one correct answer. To extend a good problem, ask, "Is the answer unique?."

To grade or not to grade. Students, particularly students who have a low opinion of mathematics and of their own mathematics ability, often find refreshing math activities that are different, fun, and not graded. Students with an interest in art, for example, who begin to see math applications in art may have an attitudinal change towards mathematics. Students who are not graded on *every* thing they do may welcome the freedom from fear of failure.

Using Special Features in *Getting Smarter Every Day*

Getting Smarter Every Day includes several types of material that present opportunities for exploring mathematics visually without specific assignments.

Grids and dot paper. Many worksheets in *Getting Smarter Every Day* emphasize drawing, sketching, designing, or problem solving. Fun Grids to Copy and Use, starting on page 102, provides several grid and dot masters. Students can use copies of these grids to work on such activities, especially to try extensions on their own. If you do not provide such grids with specific worksheets, let students know that they may request such grids if they want to use them.

Graphic images. Graphic images in *Getting Smarter Every Day* with no specific task assignment are designed to foster student appreciation of the beauty of mathematics. As previously suggested, you may use these as bulletin board material. You may also use such a graphic as a prop to ask students to bring in images from magazines, posters, or newspapers. From these contributions, you may create a bulletin board on architecture, sculpture, art, nature, and their connections to mathematics. Over the years, you may accumulate impressive files of pictures that reveal this beauty to your students.

Use of design technology. All the geometric designs in this book were created by the author on the computer using Adobe Illustrator software. Most computers have some drawing programs. You may use the graphics in *Getting Smarter Every Day* as models for students to create related images with computer drawing programs or by hand.

HOW MANY?

Count *every* one you can find.

1. How many squares?	2. How many rhombi?
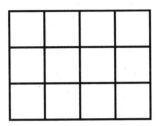	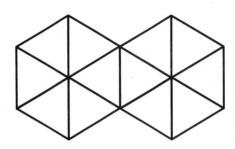
3. How many rectangles?	4. How many trapezoids?
	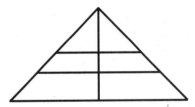
5. How many parallelograms?	6. How many parallelograms?
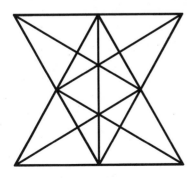	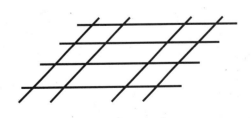

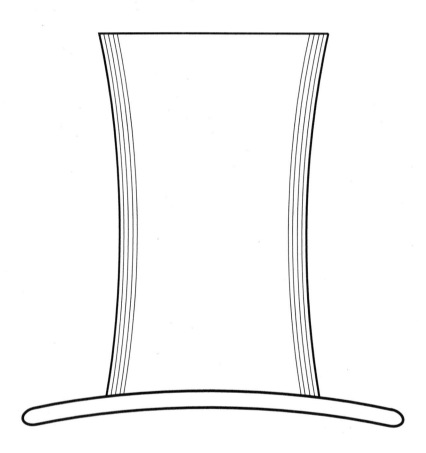

Is this hat taller than it is wide?

NUMBER PUZZLE

Use the "clues" below to write the correct number in the squares. (Don't write commas.)

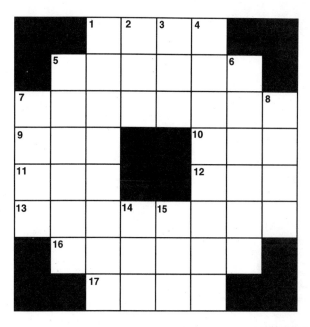

Across

1. Seven thousand six hundred forty-three
5. Four hundred twelve thousand one hundred eight
7. Thirty million six hundred thousand seven hundred one
9. Five hundred fifty-four
10. Two hundred eighty-three
11. Six hundred forty
12. Eight hundred fifty
13. Seventy-one million thirty-five thousand ninety-six
16. Nine hundred twenty thousand seven
17. Nine thousand nine hundred twenty-eight

Down

1. Seventy-one million six hundred forty thousand twenty-nine
2. Six hundred twenty
3. Four hundred ten
4. Thirty million seven hundred twenty-eight thousand eight
5. Four hundred five thousand four hundred nineteen
6. Eight hundred eight thousand five hundred ninety-seven
7. Three thousand five hundred sixty-seven
8. One thousand three hundred six
14. Three hundred nine
15. Five hundred two

SUM STRINGS

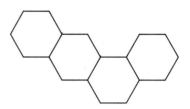

Find 16 different Sum Strings that total 22.

Fill in each set of four white hexagons with four digits (1–9) that total 22.
Don't use the same set of four numbers more than once.

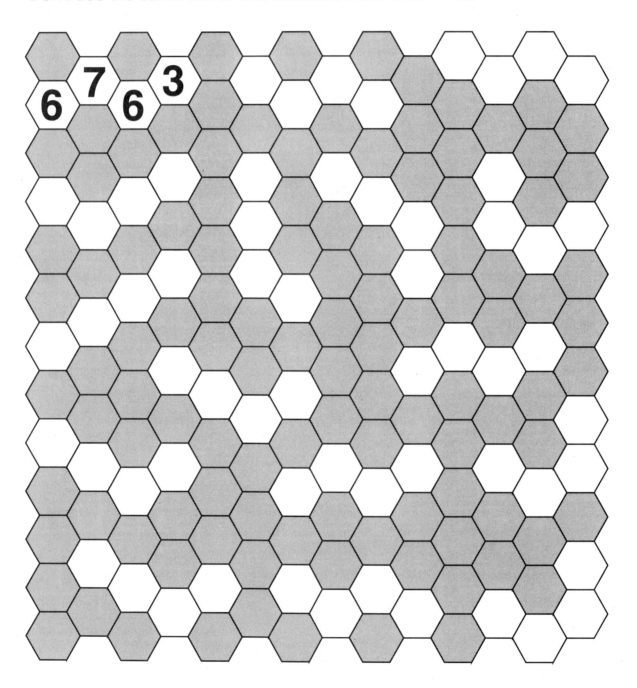

SYMMETRY

YATƎMMYS
SYMMETRY

Each of these designs is symmetrical. Notice that one half has been reflected across the dotted vertical and horizontal lines shown.

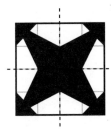 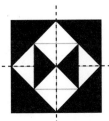 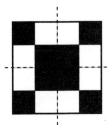 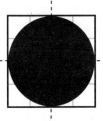

Complete each design below by reflecting it across the dotted vertical and horizontal lines shown.

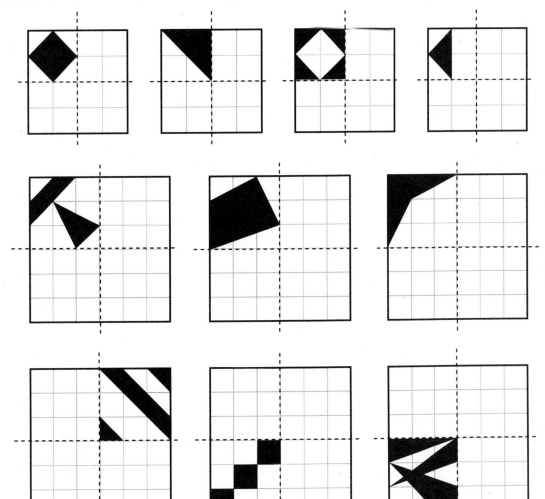

 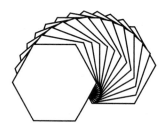 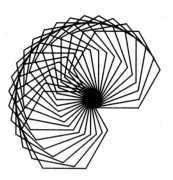

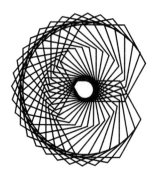 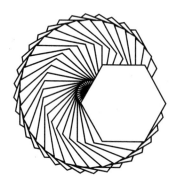 

JUGGLING DIGITS

To solve certain problems, it is important to be able to make an organized list of digits.

1. Make an organized list of *all* three-digit numbers whose digit sum is 5.

1 0 4	1 3			
1 1 3	1			
1 2	2			

2. Make an organized list of *all* three-digit numbers whose digit sum is 6.

1 0				
1 1				
1				

3. Make an organized list of *all* three-digit *odd* numbers whose digit sum is 9.

1 1				

DRAWING PATTERNS

Continue each drawing pattern.

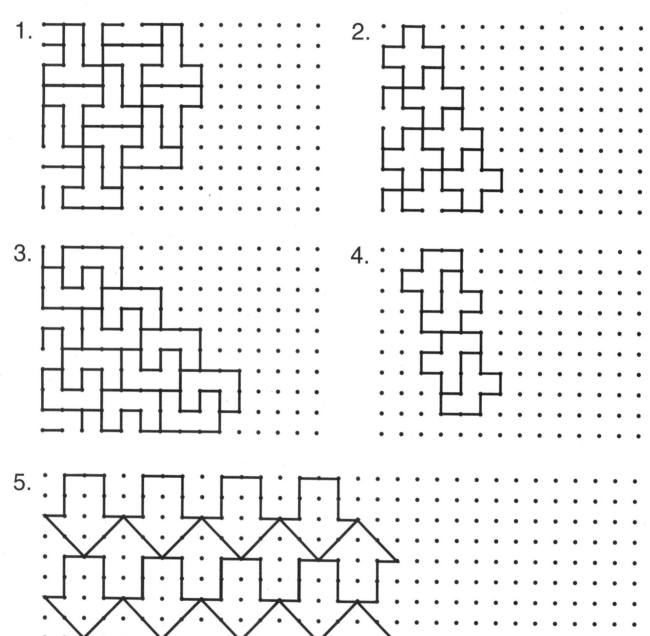

1.

2.

3.

4.

5.

SUM SHAPES

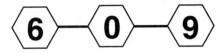

This is a sum side. Its sum is 15.
Sum shapes are made of sum sides.

In each of the five problems below,
use numbers 0, 1, 2, 3, 4, 5, 6, 7, 8
or 9 to make the sum. Don't use the
same number twice in one problem.

1.

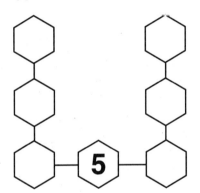

sum of 14
on each side

2.

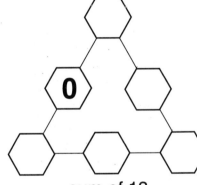

sum of 13
on each side

3.

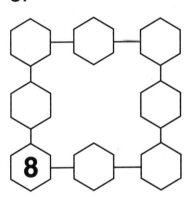

sum of 15
on each side

4.

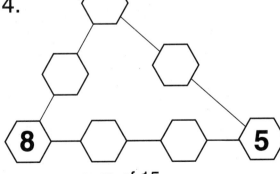

sum of 15
on each side

5.

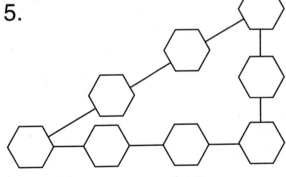

sum of 16
on each side

Regular Polygons

A *polygon* is a closed figure whose sides are line segments. A *regular polygon* is one all of whose angles are congruent (equal) and all of whose sides are congruent (equal). Some polygon names are given below.

triangle	square	pentagon	hexagon
septagon or heptagon	octagon	nonagon	decagon
undecagon	dodecagon	13-gon	14-gon
15-gon	16-gon	17-gon	18-gon
19-gon	20-gon	100-gon	■ ■ ■

NUMBER NAMES

Write each number name in words.

1. **14,657**

Fourteen thousand six hundred fifty-seven

2. **48,749**

3. **63,052**

4. **70,006**

5. **183,208**

6. **905,704**

7. **4,398,541**

8. **45,056,002**

WHICH ONE DIFFERS?

In each problem, circle the one shape that is different some way.

1. a. b. c. d. e. f. g.

2. a. b. c. d. e. f. g.

3. a. b. c. d. e. f. g.

4. a. b. c. d. e. f. g.

5. a. b. c. d. e. f. g.

6. a. b. c. d. e. f. g.

7. a. b. c. d. e. f. g.

STRAIGHT-LINE CURVES

You can draw a curve by drawing all straight lines. Here's how. Use a ruler with a straight edge. Connect the two 1's, the two 2's, the two 3's and so on. Do the same thing on the other three right angles to get a picture like the small one.

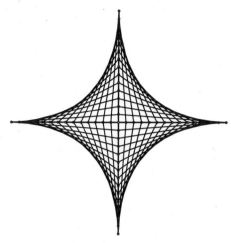

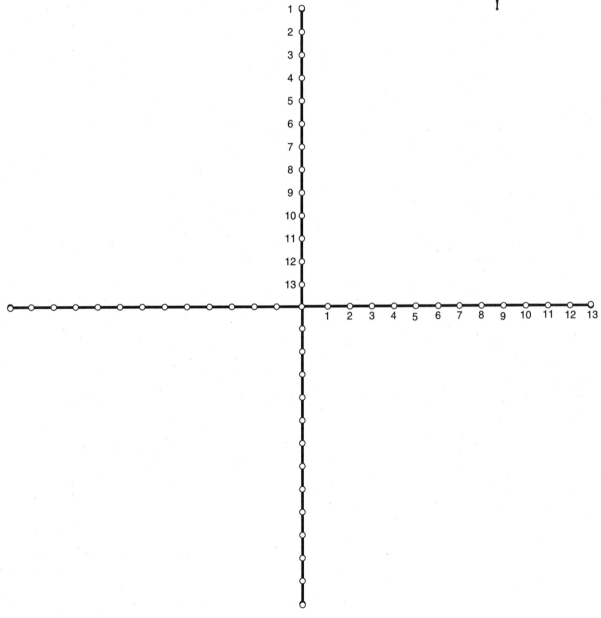

CREATING NUMBER PATTERNS

For this table of numbers, each row follows a rule. The rule appears in the black hexagon at the left of the row. At the head of each column is the value for the number (n) to use. Fill in each blank hexagon, using the corresponding rule and value for n. (Remember to do what's in parentheses first.)

rule	n = 1	n = 2	n = 3	n = 4	n = 5	n = 6	n = 7
1. n + 5		7					
2. n − 1				3			
3. n + n						12	
4. n x 4							
5. 3 x n							
6. 3 x (n +1)	6						
7. (2 x n) + 1					11		
8. n² + 2							

five-hole sand dollar

chambered nautilus

bat starfish

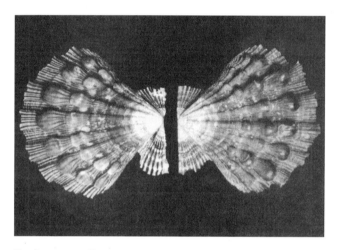

lion's paw scallop

marlin spike

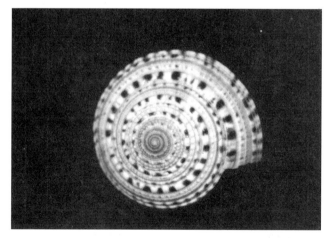

sundial

Photo source: Amy Lyn Edwards

TARGET PRACTICE

Place three of the four given numbers in the blanks to equal the target number.

1.

4
7 9
5

8

___ − ___ + ___ = **8**

2.

2
7 9
6

10

___ + ___ − ___ = **10**

3.

___ + ___ − ___ = **5**

4.

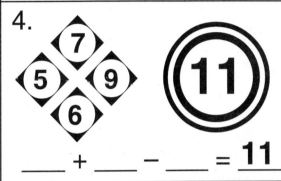

___ + ___ − ___ = **11**

5.

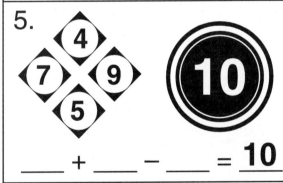

___ + ___ − ___ = **10**

6.

___ − ___ + ___ = **4**

7.

___ − ___ − ___ = **3**

8.

___ − ___ − ___ = **1**

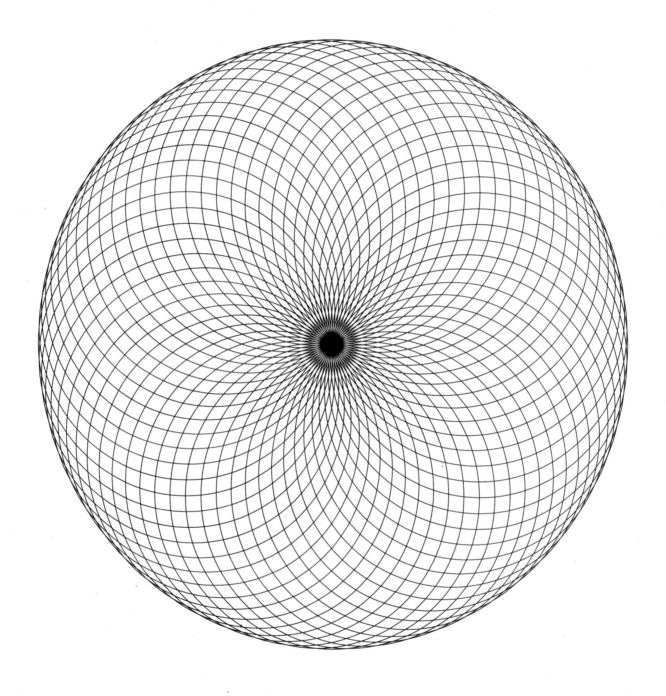

TIC-TAC-NUMBER

Use the clues to fill in the nine squares in each problem with digits 1–9 (one digit per square).

1.

a. There are no square numbers in the top or bottom rows.

b. There are no even numbers in the middle column.

c. 5 and 7 are in the bottom row.

d. 2 and 8 are in the top row.

e. All numbers in the right column are even.

f. 2 and 9 are in the left column.

g. 1 and 5 are in the middle column.

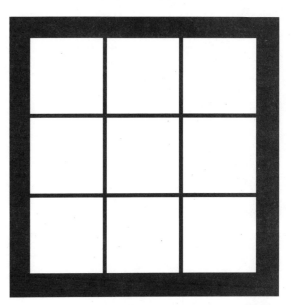

□□

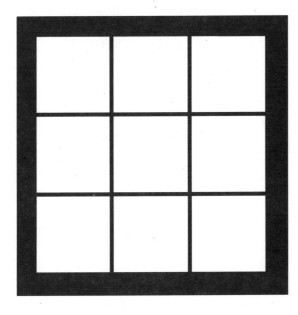

2.

a. 4, 6, 7 and 9 are corner numbers.

b. 2 and 5 are in the center row.

c. 8 and 3 are in the center column.

d. 4 and 5 are in the right column.

e. 3 and 9 are in the bottom row.

f. 2 is to the left of 8.

POLLY'S PRINT PATTERNS

Polly is a dress-material designer. Among other things, she designs patterns. Polly learned that there are 12 different shapes that can be made from six equilateral triangles. These shapes are called **hexiamonds**. The shapes are shown below.

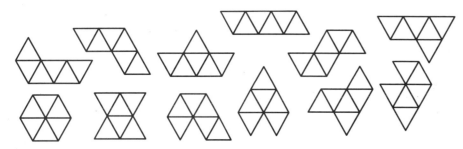

Use triangular grid paper to create tessellating patterns with each of the 12 hexiamond shapes.

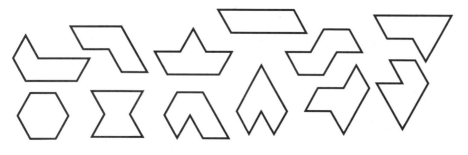

Examples

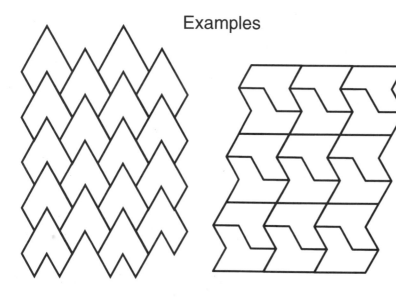

VISUAL THINKING

1. If each pattern is continued, how many white circles will be in the next row on the bottom?

   a.

   b.

   c.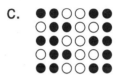

2. Which patterns will fold to make an open box?

   a.   b.   c.

   d. 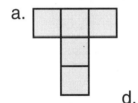   e. 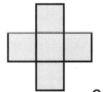   f.

   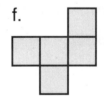

3. When this pattern is folded to form a cube, which number will be on the face opposite Face 2?

4	5	6

1	2	3

GEOMETRIC PATTERNS

Common Cents or Common Sense?

1. Would you rather have a stack of pennies 100 feet high or a stack of quarters 10 feet high?

2. Would you rather have a line of dimes 20 feet long or a line of pennies 160 feet long?

3. Would you rather get a dollar a day for 10 years or 1 cent the first day, 2 cents the second day, 4 cents the third, 8 cents the fourth, 16 cents the fifth and so on for 20 days?

SYMMETRY IN DESIGN

The 20 designs shown below are all more than 100 years old. People had their initials placed on jewelry and other personal belongings. Designers tried to form the initials so that the letters shared parts. They often made the designs quite symmetrical. What letters do you see in each design? Write your answers in the blanks at the right.

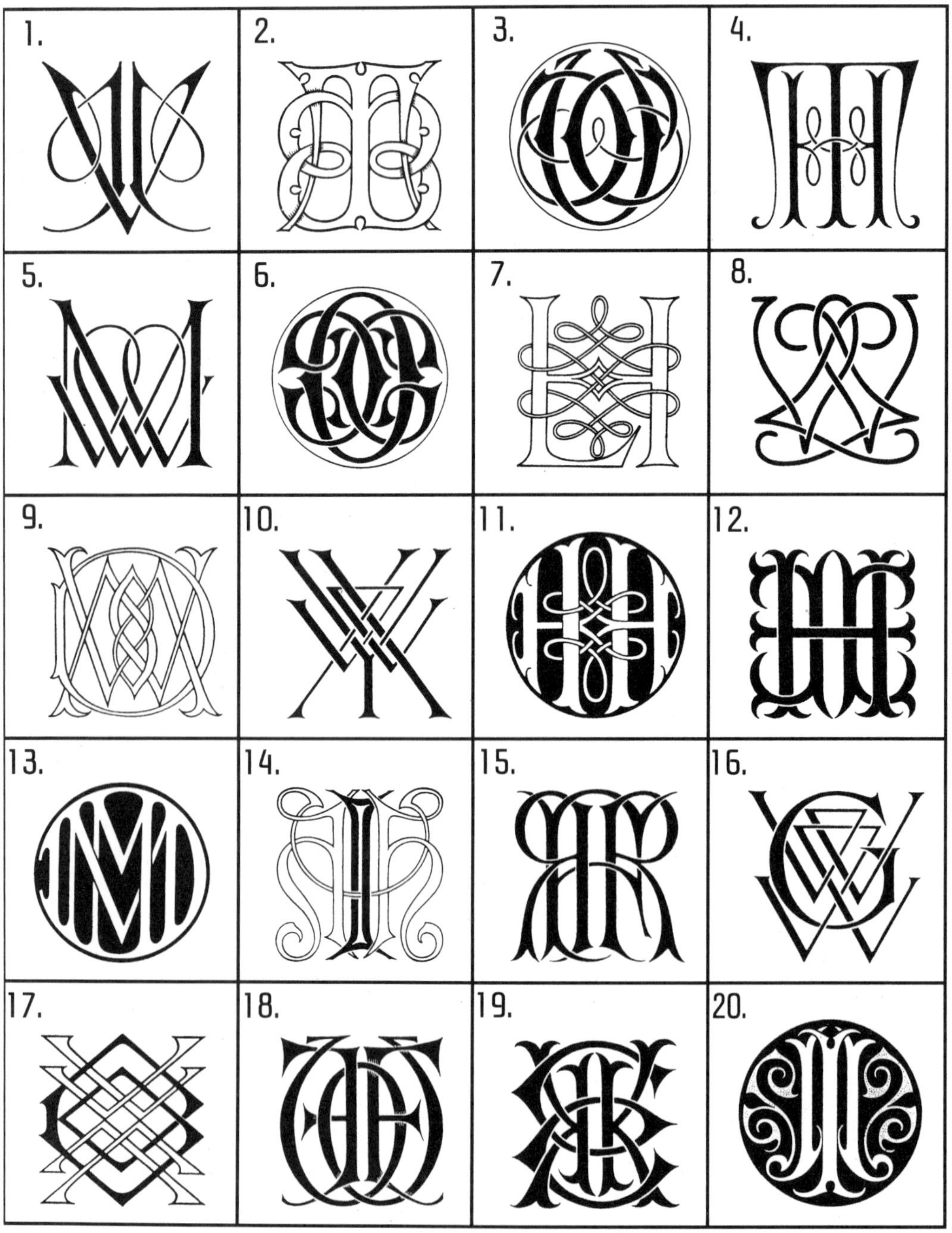

1.	2.	3.	4.	1. _____
5.	6.	7.	8.	2. _____
9.	10.	11.	12.	3. _____
13.	14.	15.	16.	4. _____
17.	18.	19.	20.	5. _____

1. _____
2. _____
3. _____
4. _____

5. _____
6. _____
7. _____
8. _____

9. _____
10. _____
11. _____
12. _____

13. _____
14. _____
15. _____
16. _____

17. _____
18. _____
19. _____
20. _____

RELATIONSHIPS

Fill in the blank to make each sentence true.

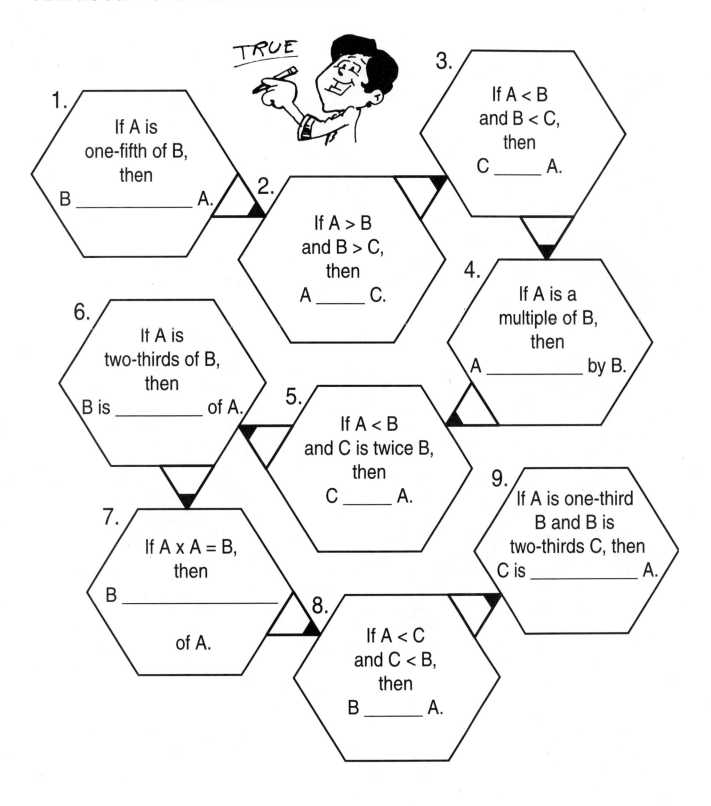

TRUE

1.
If A is
one-fifth of B,
then

B _____ A.

2.
If A > B
and B > C,
then

A _____ C.

3.
If A < B
and B < C,
then

C _____ A.

4.
If A is a
multiple of B,
then

A _____ by B.

5.
If A < B
and C is twice B,
then

C _____ A.

6.
It A is
two-thirds of B,
then

B is _____ of A.

7.
If A x A = B,
then

B _____

of A.

8.
If A < C
and C < B,
then

B _____ A.

9.
If A is one-third
B and B is
two-thirds C, then

C is _____ A.

BOX UNFOLDING

Imagine that the box at the left of each problem is unfolded into a cross pattern. Which of the four patterns makes the box shown? It may help to cut out your own pattern.

1.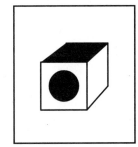

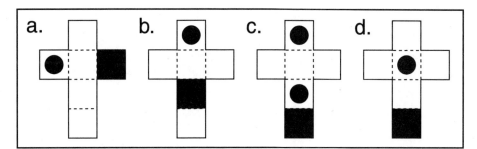

2.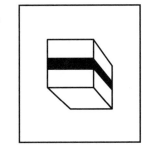

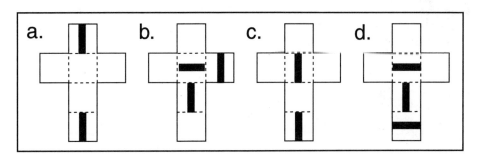

3.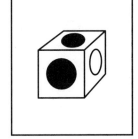

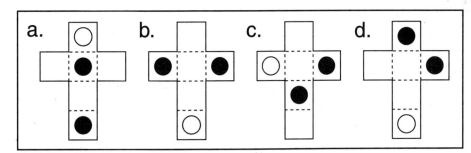

4.

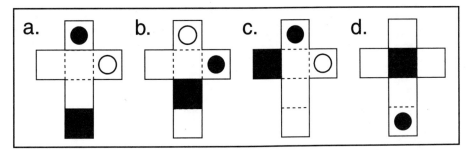

DRAWING PATTERNS

Continue each drawing pattern.

1.

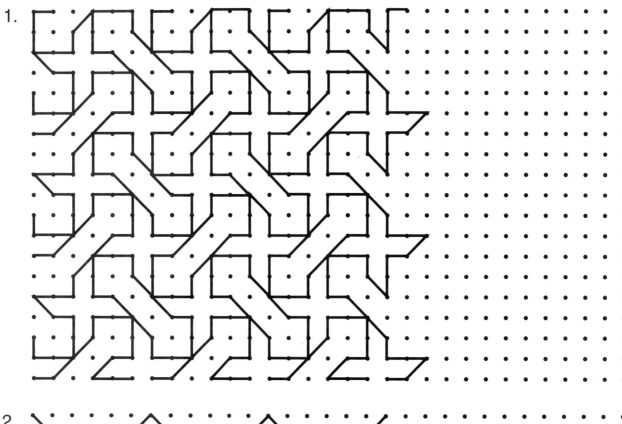

2.

PROBLEMS TO SOLVE

★★★★★★★★★★★★★★★★★★★★★★★★★★★★★★★★

1. Imagine you have a chain with 63 links. How could you cut that chain apart in three places so that you could hand a person any number of links from 1 to 63? (Each cut link also counts as a single link.)

2. A **_triangular number_** is a number that can be represented by dots arranged in the shape of a triangle. The first five triangular numbers are shown below. Looking for patterns, answer the following questions: What is the 6th triangular number? _____ the 7th? _____ the 10th? _____ the 100th? _____

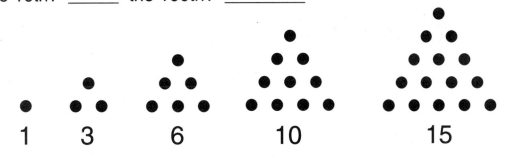

1   3   6   10   15

3. On the dot grids below, illustrate the fact that square numbers are the sum of two consecutive triangular numbers.

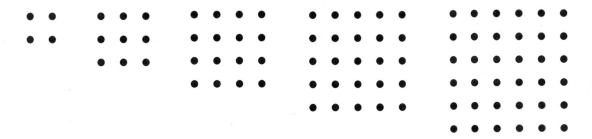

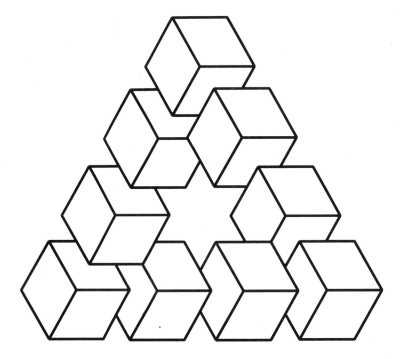

**Oscar Reutervärd made this design
in the year 1934. It shows nine cubes
in an impossible arrangement.**

HELPFUL CROSSOUTS
HELPFUL CROSSOUTS

When solving logic problems, it is often helpful to make a crossout list. As you eliminate certain possibilities from the solution, you check them off. (It is usually necessary to go back through the clues more than once.) Try using this technique in solving the two problems below.

In Race 2:

- A finished between B and E.
- B finished in front of E.
- E finished between A and C.
- A finished better than C.
- B did not win the race.

Show the order of finish in the race.

1st	2nd	3rd	4th	5th
☐	☐	☐	☐	☐
A	A	A	A	A
B	B	B	B	B
C	C	C	C	C
D	D	D	D	D
E	E	E	E	E

In Race 9:

- B came in 4th place.
- D beat C, E and two others.
- A finished ahead of E.
- F was behind D.
- C has yet to finish in the top three places in any race.
- E has never beaten F.

Show the order of finish in the race.

1st	2nd	3rd	4th	5th	6th
☐	☐	☐	☐	☐	☐
A	A	A	A	A	A
B	B	B	B	B	B
C	C	C	C	C	C
D	D	D	D	D	D
E	E	E	E	E	E
F	F	F	F	F	F

SAME SHAPES

Which five pairs are exactly the same?

_____ and _____   _____ and _____
_____ and _____   _____ and _____
_____ and _____

1.	2.	3.	4.	5.
6.	7.	8.	9.	10.
11.	12.	13.	14.	15.
16.	17.	18.	19.	20.
21.	22.	23.	24.	25.
26.	27.	28.	29.	30.

FACTOR BINGO

On the bingo card, mark as many sets as you can of 3, 4, or 5 adjacent numbers in a straight line that share a common factor. The straight line of numbers can be vertical, horizontal, or diagonal. Fill in your results below.

F-16!

B	I	N	G	O
27	28	9	15	34
35	10	125	22	25
63	14	8	21	23
75	6	39	105	66
26	19	36	77	30

Your Results

3 in a row: ☐ x 3 = _____

4 in a row: ☐ x 4 = _____

5 in a row: ☐ x 5 = _____

Total Score ☐

(23 is perfect.)

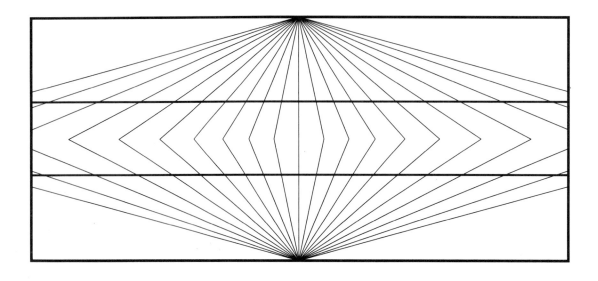

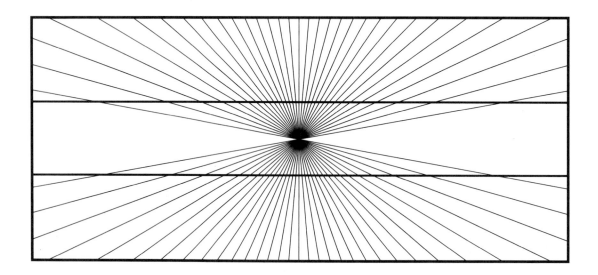

Do the two horizontal lines in each figure seem parallel?

HELPFUL CROSSOUTS

HELPFUL CROSSOUTS

When solving logic problems, it is often helpful to make a crossout list. As you eliminate certain possibilities from the solution, you cross them off. (It is usually necessary to go back through the clues more than once.) Try using this technique in solving the two problems below.

In Race 4:

- A beat D.
- E beat F.
- C beat E.
- Γ beat D.
- B came in third.
- B beat A.

Show the order of finish in the race.

1st	2nd	3rd	4th	5th	6th
□	□	□	□	□	□
A	A	A	A	A	A
B	B	B	B	B	B
C	C	C	C	C	C
D	D	D	D	D	D
E	E	E	E	E	E
F	F	F	F	F	F

In Race 7:

- No even-number horse finished in the first 3 places.
- Only one horse had the same number as its finish position.
- Number 2 did not finish last.
- The sum of the 1st and 3rd finishers was the same as the sum of the 4th and 5th.
- Number 2 beat Number 6.

Show the order of finish in the race

1st	2nd	3rd	4th	5th	6th
□	□	□	□	□	□
1	1	1	1	1	1
2	2	2	2	2	2
3	3	3	3	3	3
4	4	4	4	4	4
5	5	5	5	5	5
6	6	6	6	6	6

BEING OBSERVANT

What do we have in common?
More than one answer may be correct.

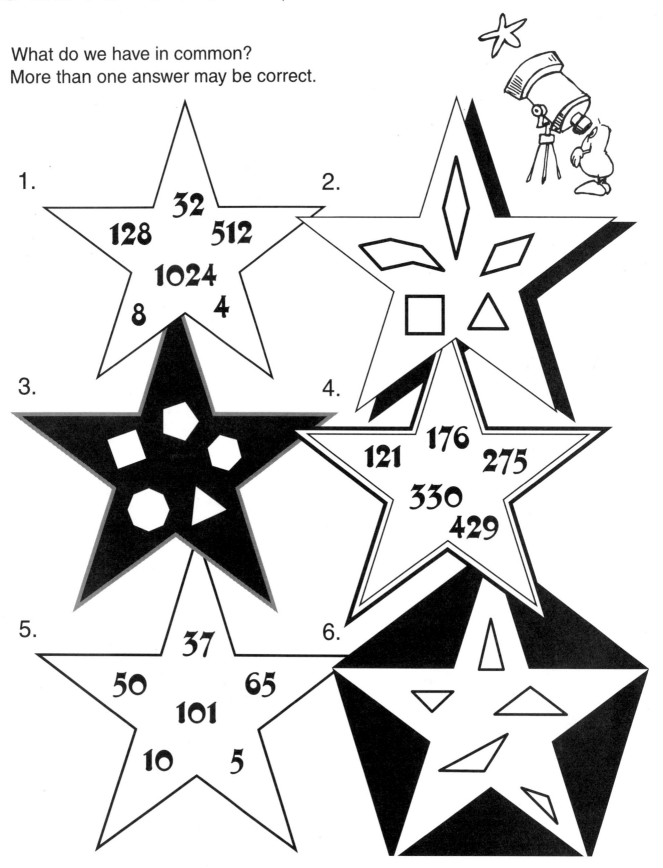

1. 32 128 512 1024 8 4

2.

3.

4. 121 176 275 330 429

5. 37 50 65 101 10 5

6.

TARGET PRACTICE

Place three of the four given numbers in
the blanks to equal the target number.

1.

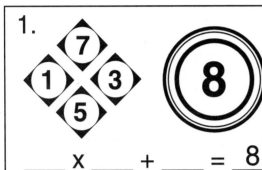

___ x ___ + ___ = __8__

2.

___ x ___ + ___ = __13__

3.

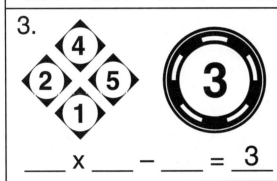

___ x ___ − ___ = __3__

4.

___ x ___ + ___ = __23__

5.

___ x ___ + ___ = __11__

6.

___ x ___ − ___ = __18__

7.

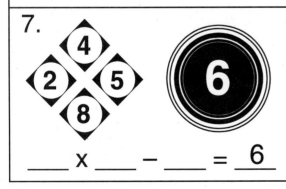

___ x ___ − ___ = __6__

8.

___ x ___ − ___ = __9__

WHEEL OF FRACTION

For each box, find the fractional part of a circle that corresponds with the fraction below the box. Place the letter of that fractional part in the box. What is the hidden message?

$\frac{2}{3}$	$\frac{1}{4}$	$\frac{5}{8}$	$\frac{1}{3}$	$\frac{7}{8}$	$\frac{1}{2}$	$\frac{1}{4}$	$\frac{5}{8}$

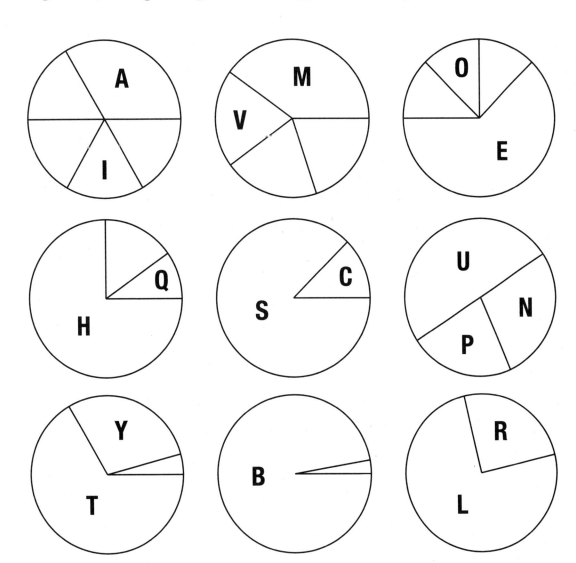

POLYOMINO PUZZLE

Polyominoes are shapes made from squares. Polyominoes made from five squares are called **pentominoes**. Five pentamino shapes are given below. Have a copy of this page made. Cut out the black shapes and try to fit all five on the 5 X 5 square.

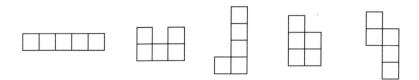

It's OK to flip the pieces over.

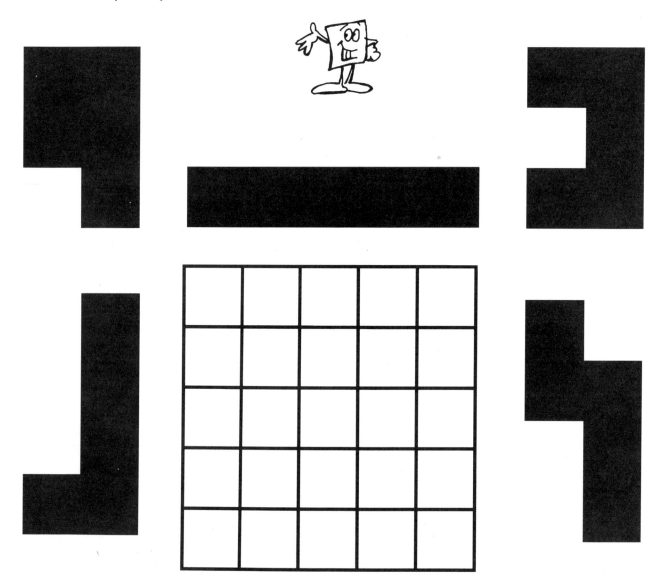

PUZZLE PIECES

---

1. Which numbered piece is not part of the design?

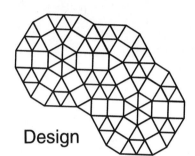

Design

a.   b.   c.

d.   e.   f.

---

2. Give the puzzle position of each lettered piece.

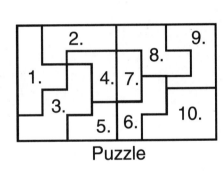

Puzzle

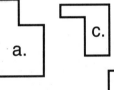

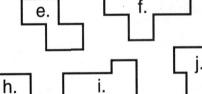

---

3. Which numbered piece does not belong to the puzzle?

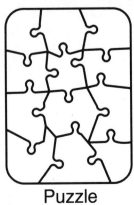

Puzzle

a.   b.    c.

d.   e.   f.

Beijing, China

Florence, Italy

Bangkok, Thailand

Taj Mahal, India

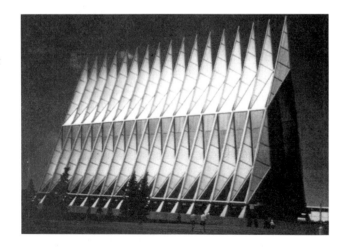

U.S. Air Force Academy, Colorado Springs, Colorado

Seoul, Korea

All photos except lower left: Christine Freeman
Lower left photo: Dale Seymour

MATCHSTICK PUZZLES

Sketch your answers in the space provided.

1. Move four matches to make exactly three congruent squares.

2. Move two matches to form four congruent rectangles.

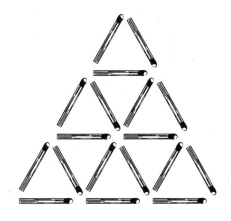  

3. Remove three matches to make six congruent equilateral triangles.

POLYOMINOES

Polyominoes are shapes made from squares. Here are some polyomino names:

Monomino	Domino	Tromino	Tetromino	Pentomino
1 square	2 squares	3 squares	4 squares	5 squares

The following shapes **are not** polyominoes. In a polyomino, squares must share an edge.

There are **12 different** pentominoes. Can you draw them all on the square grids below? (The same shape turned a different direction is not different.)

RING THINGS

1. In each square, place one number from 1 through 14 (3, 6, 7, 10 and 12 are already placed) so that the numbers in each circle total 21.

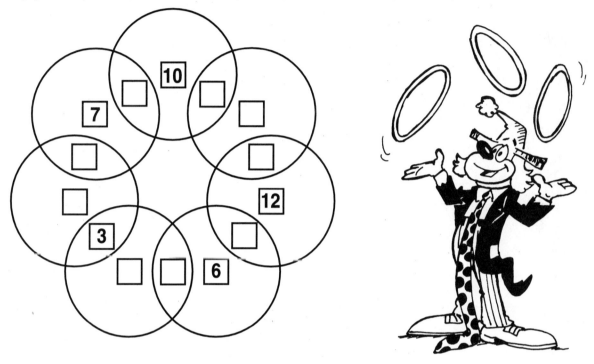

2. Which ring, when cut, will free all the others?

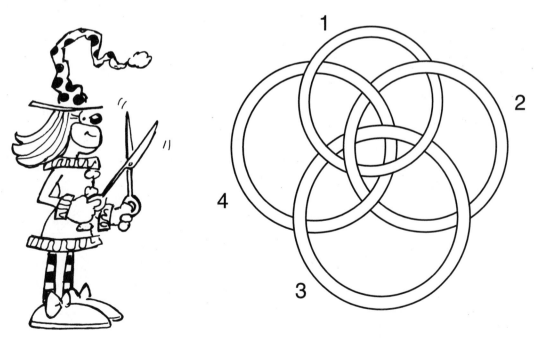

WINNING WAYS

1. In the Major League Baseball® World Series®, a team from the American League® plays a team from the National League® in up to seven games. The first team to win four games is the world champion. How many ways can a team win the series?

Win in 4 Games
WWWW

Win in 5 Games
LWWWW
WLWWW
WWLWW
_____

Win in 6 Games
LLWWWW
LWLWWW
LWWLWW
LWWWLW
WLLWWW
WLWLWW
_____
_____
_____
_____

Win in 7 Games

2. If each team has a 50-50 chance of winning any game, what is the probability that the National League team will win the World Series in four games? _____

3. What is the probability that the series will be won in five games? _____

4. What is the probability that the American League team will win in six games? _____

5. What are the chances that the series will go to seven games? _____

6. What are the chances that the National League team will win in six games or more? _____

7. Name some businesses that would like the World Series to last seven games.

BASIC GEOMETRIC CONSTRUCTIONS

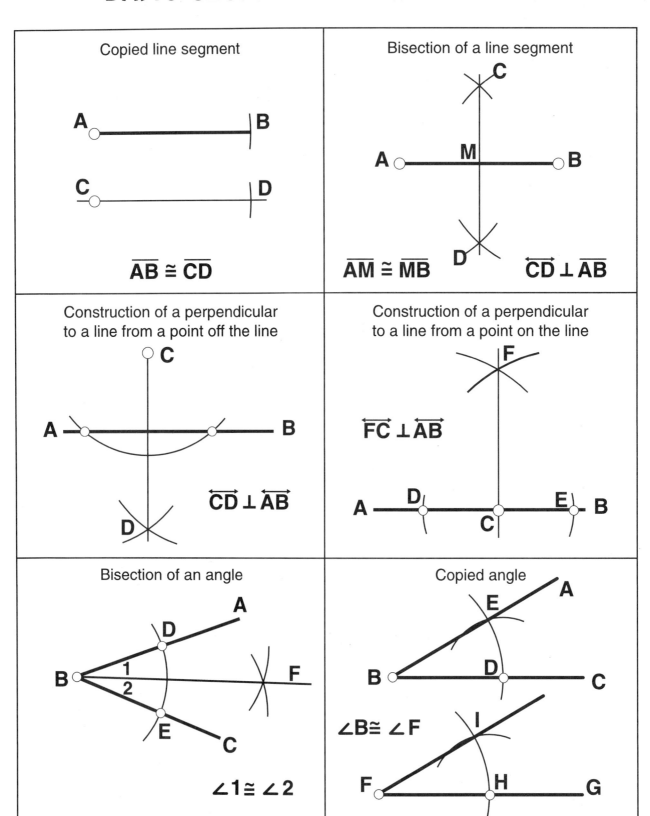

Copied line segment

$$\overline{AB} \cong \overline{CD}$$

Bisection of a line segment

$$\overline{AM} \cong \overline{MB}$$ $$\overleftrightarrow{CD} \perp \overline{AB}$$

Construction of a perpendicular to a line from a point off the line

$$\overleftrightarrow{CD} \perp \overleftrightarrow{AB}$$

Construction of a perpendicular to a line from a point on the line

$$\overleftrightarrow{FC} \perp \overleftrightarrow{AB}$$

Bisection of an angle

$$\angle 1 \cong \angle 2$$

Copied angle

$$\angle B \cong \angle F$$

CAN YOU CONSTRUCT THESE?

Use either compass and straight edge or a computer drawing program.

STAR DESIGNS

MATHEMATICS IS THE STUDY OF PATTERN.

CREATING A DESIGN

The steps below show how a designer makes a five-pointed star.

1.

Draw a circle.

2.

Draw a radius
of the circle.

3.

Rotate the radius 1/5 of
a complete rotation (72°).

4.

Repeat the rotation,
dividing circle into fifths.

5.

Erase the circle.
It was only a helper.

6.

Connect the endpoints of
all non-adjacent radii.

7.

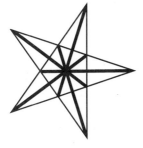

Extend each of the
five radii.

8.

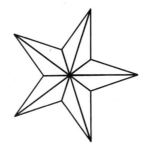

Erase lines.

9.

Fill in every other triangle,
and rotate figure.

CONSTRUCTING A REGULAR PENTAGON

1. Draw a circle and a diameter of that circle, **AB**.

2. Construct another diameter, **CD**, the perpendicular bisector of **AB**.

3. Bisect **OB**. Label the midpoint **M**.

4. Using **M** as a center and **CM** as a radius, draw an arc intersecting **AO** at **E**.

5. **CE** is the required length of one side of the inscribed regular pentagon.

6. On the circle, mark five arcs with radius **CE.** Connect their intersections to form the regular pentagon.

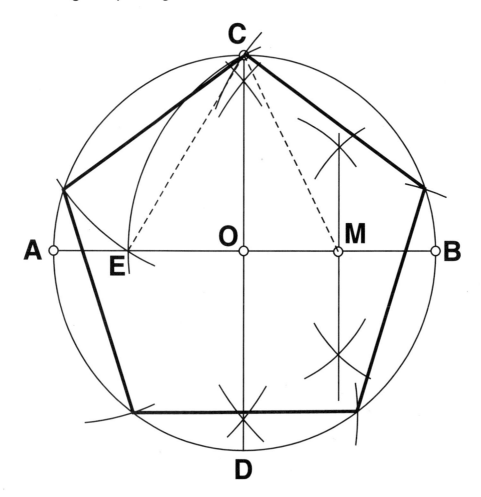

BOX FOLDING

Imagine that the pattern at the left of each problem is folded into a cube. Which of the four cubes could be made from the pattern shown? It may help to cut out your own pattern.

1.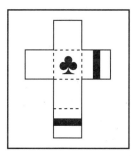

   a.   b.   c.   d.

2.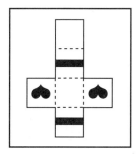

   a.   b.   c.   d.

3.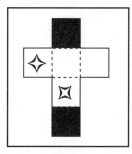

   a.   b.   c.   d.

4.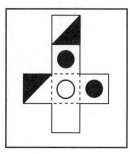

   a.   b.   c.   d.

SQUARE PUZZLE

Have a copy of this page made. Cut out each of the six shapes below and place the pieces together in the shape of a square. You can also make a cross, a parallelogram, a triangle, and a trapezoid. Be sure to use all 6 pieces on each puzzle.

WHO AM I?

1. I am a prime number. Each of my two digits is prime. The sum of my two digits is prime.

Who am I?

2.

I am a palindromic number. That means I read the same forwards and backwards. The sum of my two digits is one less than a square.

Who am I?

3. I'm a three-digit number. Cover up my units digit and you see a square number. Cover up my hundreds digit and you also see a square number. The sum of my digits is composite.

Who am I?

4.

I am not a prime number. I am a two-digit odd number. Each of my digits is composite. The sum of my digits is prime. The difference of my digits is prime.

Who am I?

SEEING INTO THINGS

What can you do with a "W"?

You can turn it upside down.

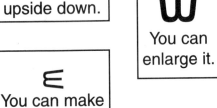
You can enlarge it.

You can shrink it.

You can stretch it.

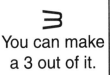
You can squash it.

You can make an E out of it.

You can outline it.

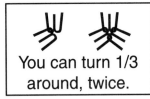
You can make a 3 out of it.

You can copy it over and over and over.

What can you do with two or more "W"s?

You can make two into a white "H".

You can turn 1/3 around, twice.

You can turn 1/3 around, twice.

SUM SHAPES

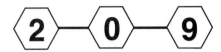

This is a sum side. Its sum is 11. You can use sum sides to build sum shapes.

In each problem below, use numbers 0, 1, 2, 3, 4, 5, 6, 7, 8 or 9 to make the sum. Don't use the same number twice in one problem.

1. Make a sum shape of 14 on each side.

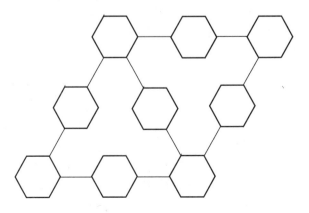

2. Make a sum shape of 15 on each side.

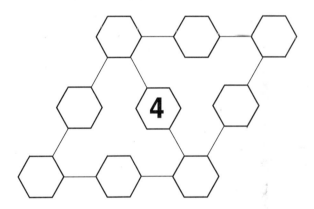

3. Make a sum shape of 16 on each side.

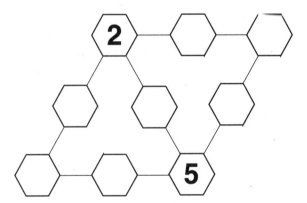

4. Make a sum shape of 17 on each side.

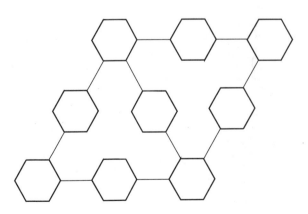

SAME SHAPES

In each problem, find the three pairs of shapes that are exactly the same.

_____ & _____ / _____ & _____ / _____ & _____   _____ & _____ / _____ & _____ / _____ & _____

1.
a.	b.	c.
d.	e.	f.
g.	h.	i.
j.	k.	l.
m.	n.	o.
p.	q.	r.
s.	t.	u.
v.	w.	x.
y.	z.	*

2.
a.	b.	c.
d.	e.	f.
g.	h.	i.
j.	k.	l.
m.	n.	o.
p.	q.	r.
s.	t.	u.
v.	w.	x.
y.	z.	*

GROUPING NUMBERS

I go first!

Parentheses say,
"I go first!"
$(7 \times 3) - 2 = 19$
$7 \times (3 - 2) = 7$

Place parentheses as needed to make each sentence true.

1. $5 + 3 \times 4 = 32$

2. $5 + 3 \times 4 = 17$

3. $12 \div 4 - 2 = 1$

4. $12 \div 4 - 2 = 6$

5. $15 - 5 - 2 = 8$

6. $15 - 5 - 2 = 12$

7. $3 \times 8 - 2 = 22$

8. $3 \times 8 - 2 = 18$

9. $3 \times 6 + 1 = 21$

10. $3 \times 6 + 1 = 19$

11. $12 \div 2 \times 2 = 12$

12. $12 \div 2 \times 2 = 3$

STAR DESIGNS

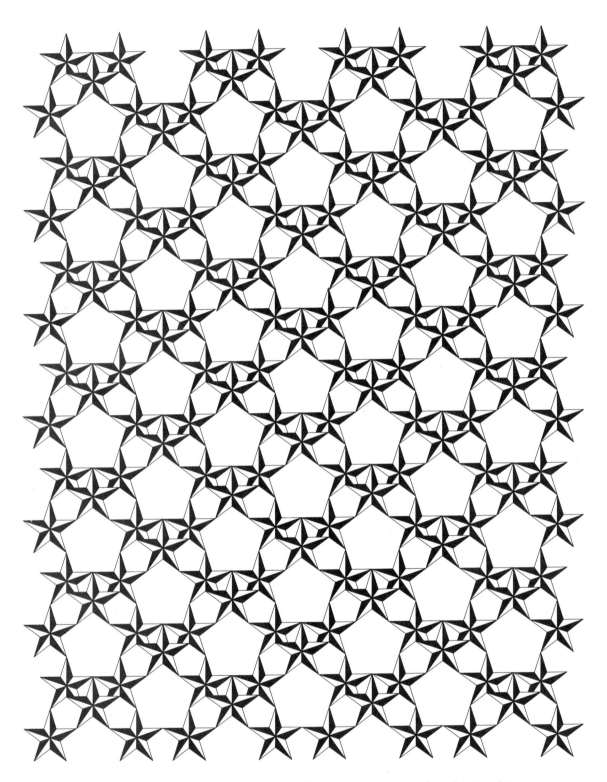

MATHEMATICS IS THE STUDY OF PATTERN.

HOW MANY?

Count *every* one you can find.

---

1. How many squares?

2. How many rectangles?

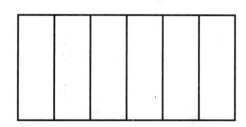

---

3. How many trapezoids?

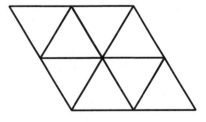

4. How many parallelograms?

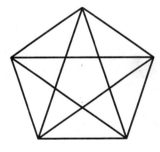

---

5. How many parallelograms?

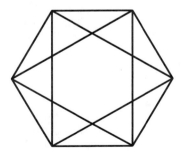

6. How many regular hexagons?

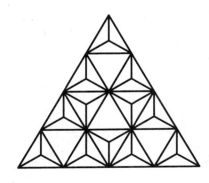

WHAT *FRACTIONAL* PART?

Using the first rectangle below, which has dividing lines drawn, figure what fraction of each rectangle is black. Write your answer as a fraction in lowest terms.

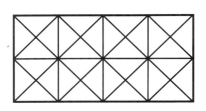

1. _____

2. _____

3. _____

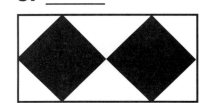

4. _____

5. _____

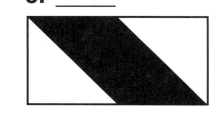

6. _____

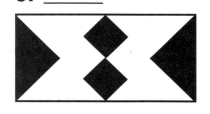

7. _____

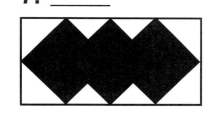

8. _____

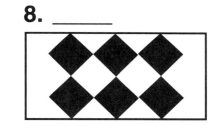

9. _____

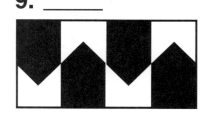

10. _____

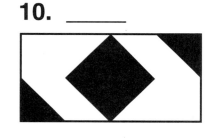

11. _____

12. _____

13. _____

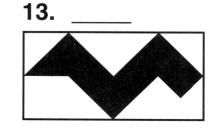

14. _____

ALPHA-NUMERIC PUZZLES

Alpha-numeric puzzles are computation problems written in letters instead of numerals. To make a solution, you'll need to figure out which numeral each letter represents. If a letter appears more than once, it represents the same number. One puzzle may have several different correct answers.

J-U-D-Y

1.

```
    E
    Z
 + A S
 -----
  P I E
```

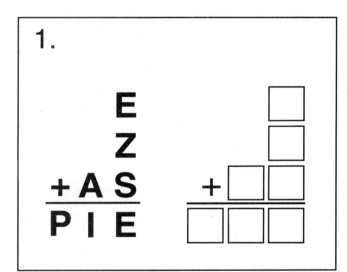

2.

```
   O N E
   O N E
 + O N E
 -------
 T R E Y
```

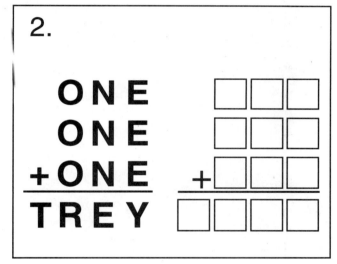

3.

```
  O O
  S A
  C A N
 +   U
 -----
  S E E
```

4.

```
   W I N
 + T H E
 -------
 G A M E
```

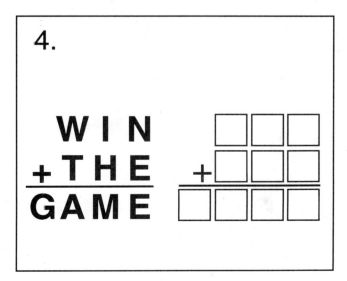

DRAWING ANGLES

Angle and rotation measure is measured in units called **degrees**. A complete rotation covers 360 degrees. You can draw angles of a specific measure using a protractor. In the example below, you see two different ways to draw an 80-degree angle with a protractor. Both are correc

We read the angles shown as Angle AOB and Angle COD. The **vertex** of the angle is the point that lies on both sides of the angle. It is always read and written between the other two letters.

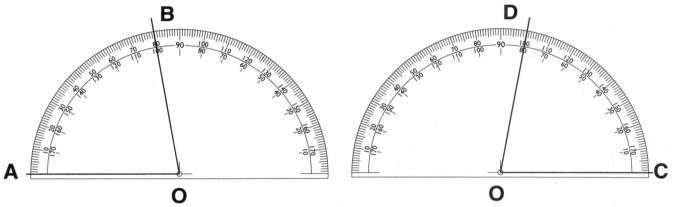

On the chart below, use a protractor to draw the 8 angles listed. The first two points of each angle lie on the line near the bottom of the page. After you measure the angle, draw the second line through the row of lower-case alphabet letters. Those letters will help your teacher gauge the accuracy of your angles quickly. Label, with a capital letter, the third point. The first angle is done as an example.

1. ∠ABC = 120°   2. ∠XDE = 130°   3. ∠AFG = 65°   4. ∠XHI = 45°
5. ∠AJK = 87°   6. ∠XLM = 88°   7. ∠ANO = 145°   8. ∠XPQ = 93°

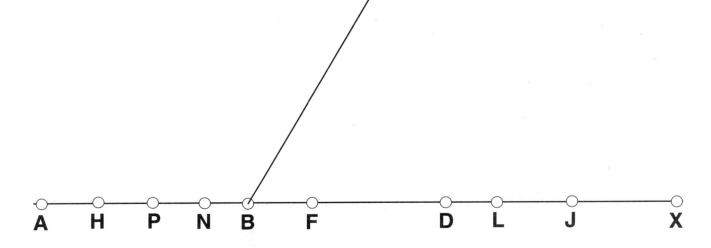

Kaleidoscope designs are made from mirror reflections.

KALEIDOSCOPE DESIGN

A kaleidoscope design contains mirror symmetry on each of the three lines connecting opposite vertices of the regular hexagons. Design some kaleidoscope patterns of your own in the grids provided.

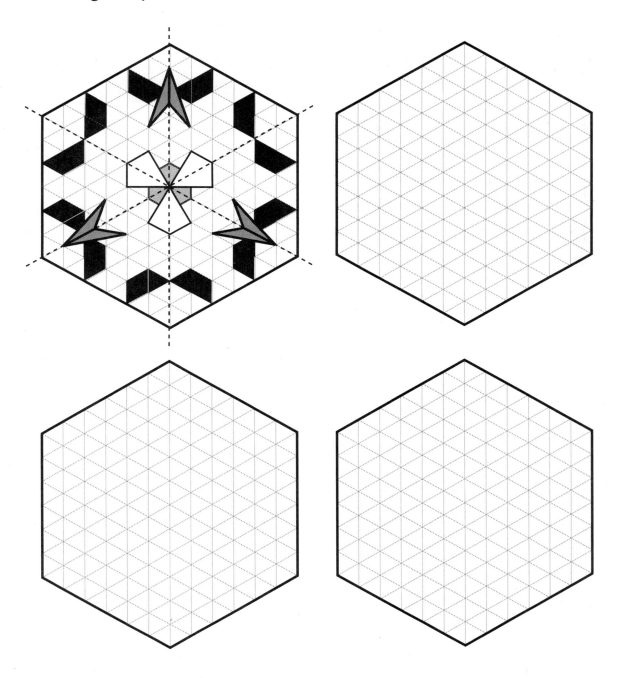

LOGOS

Logos are designs that identify a product or company. Logos are often geometric. Designers frequently design logos to be simple and symmetrical. Sometimes the company's initials or their products are in the logo.

Here are some examples of typical logos.

Simple, Symmetric Geometric

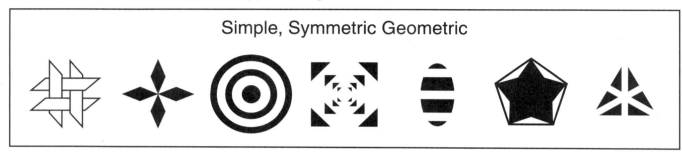

Company's Initials

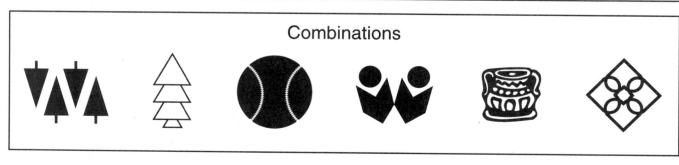

Company's Product or Name

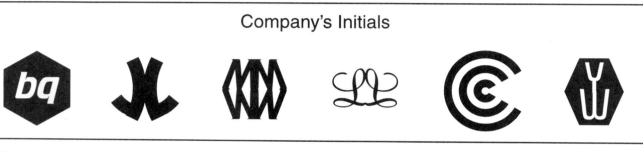

Combinations

Look through newspapers and magazine to find ten good examples of the properties shown above. Design a logo of your own.

VISUAL THINKING

1. A square has four lines of symmetry.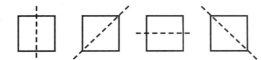

   How many lines of symmetry does each of these figures have?

   a.   b.   c.   d.

   e.   f. 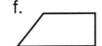   g.   h.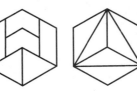

2. There are four nesting boxes.

   The blue box is inside the yellow box.
   The green box is inside the red box.
   The blue box is outside the green box.
   The yellow box is outside the red box.

   a. Which box is the smallest?
   b. Which box is the largest?

3. Each of these regular hexagons is divided into 6 equal areas.

   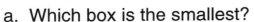

   On a separate sheet of paper, show at least 6 ways to divide a square into four equal areas.

   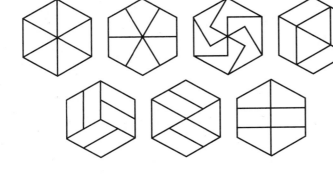

THE H PUZZLE

Have a copy of this page made. Cut out each of the six shapes. Place the pieces together in the shape of an H.

Digit Dilemmas

1. What is the largest three-digit number that is divisible by 17?

2. What is the smallest palindromic square number greater than 1?

3. There are 21 three-digit square numbers. Only one of these contains three prime digits. What is that number?

4. The number 264 is formed by three consecutive even digits. It is also divisible by 2, 4 and 6. What is the largest three-digit number that is evenly divisible by three consecutive even numbers or consecutive odd numbers and is also divisible by each of its digits?

LETTER SYMMETRY

1. Circle each letter M that has vertical symmetry.

1	2	3	4	5	6	7	8	9	10
M	M	M	M	M	M	M	M	M	M

11	12	13	14	15	16	17	18	19	20
M	M	M	M	M	M	M	M	M	M

21	22	23	24	25	26	27	28	29	30
M	M	M	M	M	M	M	M	M	M

2. Circle each letter E that has horizontal symmetry.

1	2	3	4	5	6	7	8	9	10
E	E	E	E	E	E	E	E	E	E

11	12	13	14	15	16	17	18	19	20
E	E	E	E	E	E	E	E	E	E

21	22	23	24	25	26	27	28	29	30
E	E	E	E	E	E	E	E	E	E

3. Circle each letter H that has both horizontal and vertical symmetry.

1	2	3	4	5	6	7	8	9	10
H	H	H	H	H	H	H	H	H	H

11	12	13	14	15	16	17	18	19	20
H	H	H	H	H	H	H	H	H	H

21	22	23	24	25	26	27	28	29	30
H	H	H	H	H	H	H	H	H	H

BOX UNFOLDING

Imagine that the box at the left of each problem is unfolded in a cross pattern. Which of the four patterns is correct to make the box that is shown? It may help to cut out your own pattern.

1.
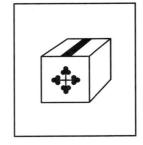
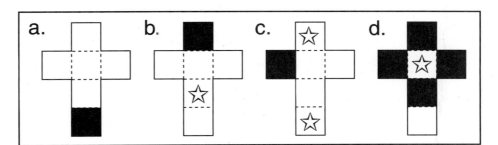

2.

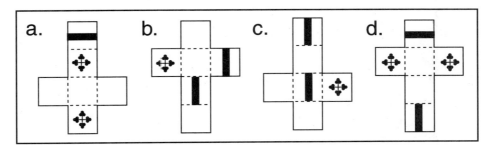

3.

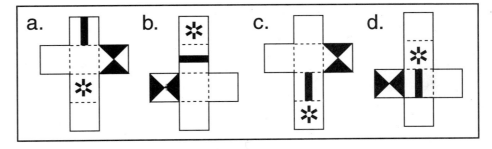

4.

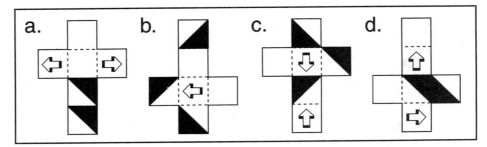

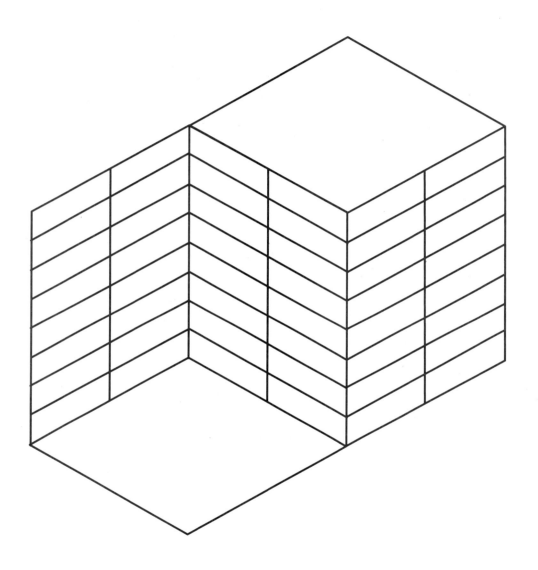

PROBLEMS TO SOLVE

★★★★★★★★★★★★★★★★★★★★★★★★★★★★★★★

1. Suppose that 3 and 8 are the only individual
   scores that can be made in a certain game.
   What scores are impossible to make in
   this game?

2. The sum of the digits of an odd two-digit prime number is 11.
   The tens digit is greater than the ones digit.
   What is the number? _____

3. It is believed that every even number greater than four can be written
   as the sum of two prime numbers. For example:

$$12 = 5 + 7$$
$$68 = 7 + 61$$

Find prime-number sums for each even number from 30 through 56.

30 = _____   44 = _____

32 = _____   46 = _____

34 = _____   48 = _____

36 = _____   50 = _____

38 = _____   52 = _____

40 = _____   54 = _____

42 = _____   56 = _____

TESSELLATING

Every parallelogram will **tessellate** the plane. You can get more interesting shapes by modifying the parallelograms. You can modify one side and then slide (translate) that change to the opposite side. The parallelogram no longer looks the same. It does, however, tessellate.

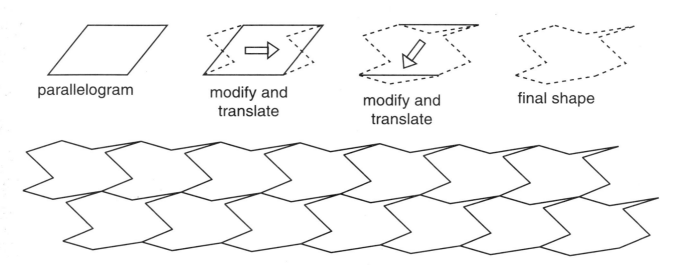

parallelogram

modify and translate

modify and translate

final shape

Try this technique of modifying the opposite sides of a parallelogram on the dot paper below. Then show that your shape tessellates.

STRAIGHT EIGHT

Roger played the game of "straight 8." In the game, you use each of the digits 1–9 once in a 3 X 3 grid. The object is to arrange the digits in the squares to get the greatest number of strings that total the "target number." Roger's target was 14. He did well. He got 5 strings of 3 that totaled 14.

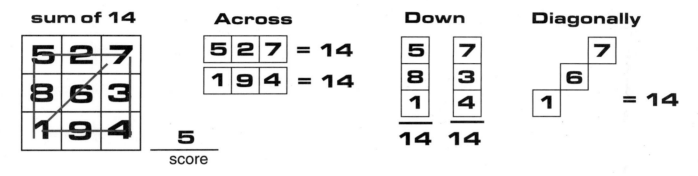

What are your best scores in the six "straight 8" games below?

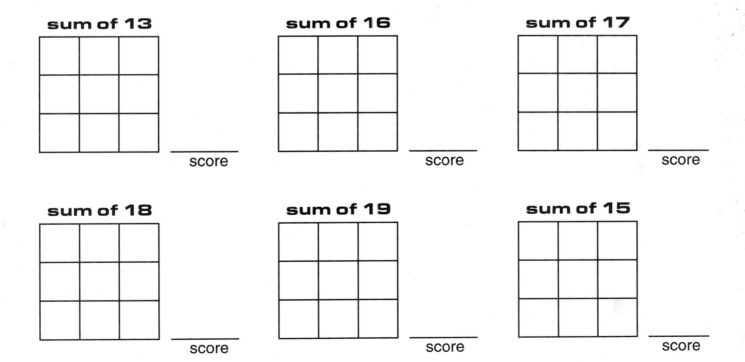

WHAT CAN YOU DO WITH A *WORD*?

You can:

rotate it	shrink it	enlarge it	reflect it
reflect it	sheer it	outline it	interrupt it
smash it	stretch it	shadow it	reverse it

Or you could:

Use geometric and graphic tools on your computer to play with your name.

WHAT DIRECTION?

Kansas City is located south and west of Chicago. We say that Kansas City is southwest of Chicago. Chicago is located northeast of Kansas City. St. Louis is considered east of Denver, since it is closer to east than it is to southeast.

Seattle
Salt Lake City
San Francisco
Denver
Chicago
New York
Kansas City
St Louis
San Diego
Atlanta
Dallas
New Orleans
Miami

Give the most accurate directions.

1. Salt Lake is _____ of Seattle.
2. San Francisco is _____ of San Diego.
3. New York is _____ of Chicago.
4. San Francisco is _____ of St. Louis.
5. New Orleans is _____ of Dallas.
6. Seattle is _____ of San Francisco.
7. Atlanta is _____ of New Orleans.
8. Denver is _____ of Dallas.

Which is the longer flight?

9. a. New York–Dallas–San Diego or
   b. Salt Lake–Chicago–Miami? _____

10. a. New Orleans–Kansas City–San Francisco or
    b. San Diego–Denver–Atlanta? _____

It is about 3000 miles from New York to San Francisco. Estimate the following distances to the nearest 100 miles.

11. Chicago to San Francisco _____
12. Denver to New York _____
13. Atlanta to Seattle _____
14. Denver to Chicago to Miami _____

GEOMETRIC PATTERNS

ALPHA-NUMERIC PUZZLES

Alpha-numeric puzzles are computation problems written in letters instead of numerals. To make a solution, you'll need to figure out which numeral each letter represents. If a letter appears more than once, it represents the same number. One puzzle may have several different correct answers.

1.

```
  W H A T   ☐☐☐☐
+   N O S   ☐☐☐
         + ☐☐☐
  W O R K   ☐☐☐☐
```

2.

```
  A D D      ☐☐☐
  M E         ☐☐
+ U P       +  ☐☐
  S U M      ☐☐☐
```

3.

```
  O N E      ☐☐☐
+ M O R E   ☐☐☐☐
  T I M E   ☐☐☐☐
```

4.

```
  N O T      ☐☐☐
+ S O         ☐☐
            +  ☐☐
  E A Z Y   ☐☐☐☐
```

TARGET PRACTICE

Use three of the four numbers to write a number sentence equaling the target number. Use parentheses to show what should be done first.

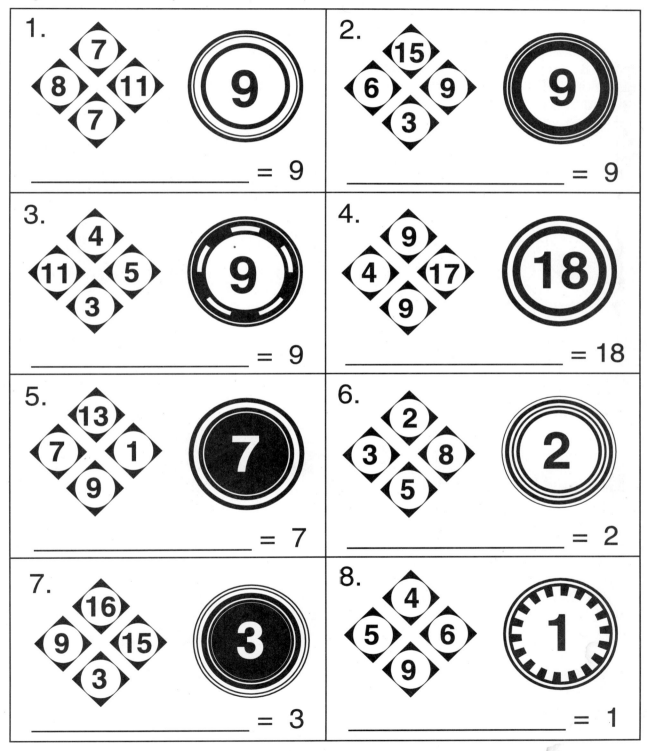

1. 7, 8, 11, 7 → 9

_____ = 9

2. 15, 6, 9, 3 → 9

_____ = 9

3. 4, 11, 5, 3 → 9

_____ = 9

4. 9, 4, 17, 9 → 18

_____ = 18

5. 13, 7, 1, 9 → 7

_____ = 7

6. 2, 3, 8, 5 → 2

_____ = 2

7. 16, 9, 15, 3 → 3

_____ = 3

8. 4, 5, 6, 9 → 1

_____ = 1

EIGHT CONGRUENT SQUARES

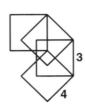 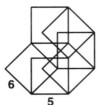 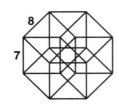

This design, formed by 8 congruent squares, is the basis for all the three-dimensional drawings below. On the lines at the bottom of the page, make other design patterns from the 8-square design.

FRACTION SIZE

Complete the fraction value for each marked circle on the number lines below. For each number line, use only digits in the corresponding left-hand box. You may use those digits more than once.

1. 1, 2, 3, 4

0 ‒ $\dfrac{1}{\Box}$ ‒ $\dfrac{\Box}{\Box}$ ‒ 1 ‒ $\dfrac{4}{\Box}$ $\dfrac{\Box}{2}$ ‒ 2

2. 1, 2, 3, 4, 5

0 ‒ $\dfrac{\Box}{\Box}$ ‒ $\dfrac{\Box}{\Box}$ ‒ $\dfrac{\Box}{\Box}$ ‒ 1 ‒ $\dfrac{\Box}{\Box}$ ‒ 2

3. 3, 5, 7, 9

0 ‒ $\dfrac{\Box}{\Box}$ ‒ $\dfrac{\Box}{\Box}$ ‒ 1 ‒ $\dfrac{7}{\Box}$ ‒ $\dfrac{\Box}{5}$ ‒ 2

4. 1, 5, 6, 8

0 $\dfrac{\Box}{\Box}$ ‒ $\dfrac{\Box}{\Box}$ ‒ 1 ‒ $\dfrac{\Box}{\Box}$ ‒ $\dfrac{\Box}{\Box}$ ‒ 2

5. 6, 7, 9, 10

0 ‒ $\dfrac{\Box}{\Box}$ ‒ $\dfrac{\Box}{\Box}$ 1 $\dfrac{\Box}{\Box}$ ‒ $\dfrac{\Box}{\Box}$ ‒ 2

Starburst by John Robinson
Used by permission of Edition Limitée.

LICENSE TO COUNT

Using three letters at the beginning of a license plate, 26 different letters can be used in each position. An organized list of all possible arrangements would start: AAA, AAB, AAC, AAD, AAE, and end with ZZY, ZZZ. A short-cut method is: 26 X 26 X 26. The total possible arrangements would be 17,576.

Using three digits, you would have: 000, 001, 002, 003, . . . 998, 999. A short-cut method is: 10 X 10 X 10. If you used 3 letters and 3 numerals, with 17,576 letter and 1,000 numeral combinations, you would have 26 X 26 X 26 X 10 X 10 X10, or 17,576,000 different license plates.

Would this be enough plates for all the cars in your state? _____
About how many people live in your state? _____

1. How many different plates could be made using two letters and four digits?

   _____

2. How many different plates could be made using two letters and five digits?

   _____

3. How many different plates could be made using only one of the digits 1,2 or 3, followed by three letters and three digits?

   _____

GEOMETRIC PATTERNS

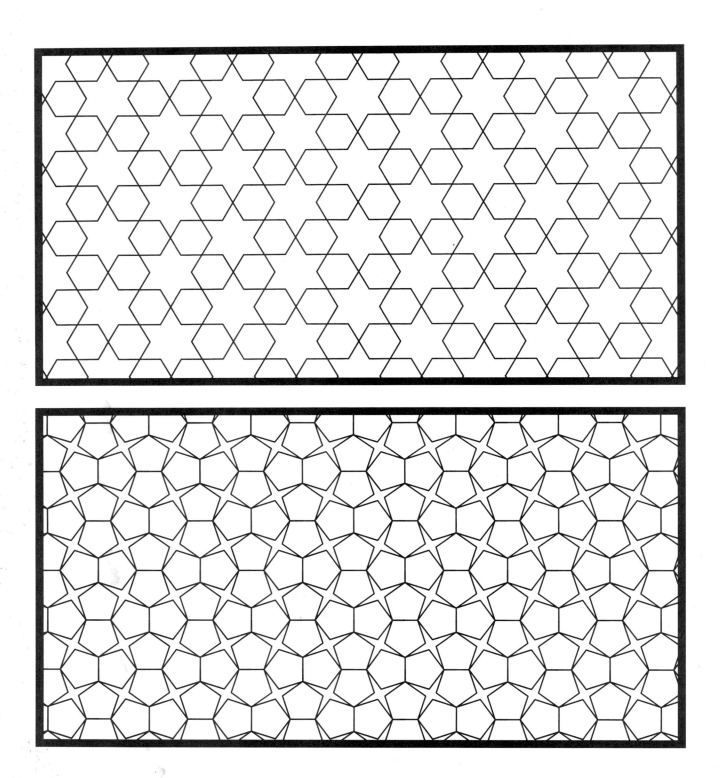

VISUAL THINKING

1. Find two designs that are exactly alike.

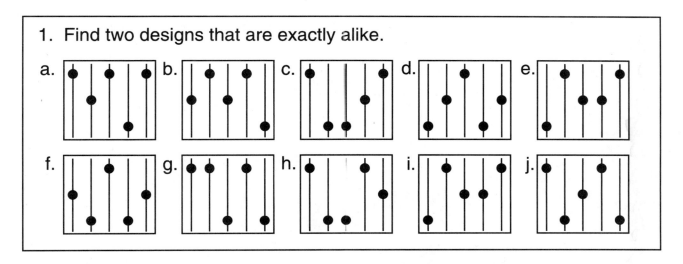

2. Draw three overlapping circles. Place 3 X's so that each circle contains three X's. Repeat the problem using four X's, five X's, six X's, and seven X's. (Each time, have three X's in each circle.)

3. This is Box A and a pattern for making it.

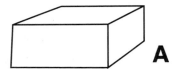

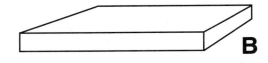

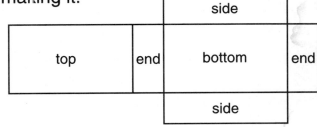

Draw a pattern for Box B on a separate sheet of paper.

PASCAL'S TRIANGLE

This useful triangle has many practical applications. The triangle continues infinitely.

Pascal's Triangle contains many patterns. What patterns can you find?

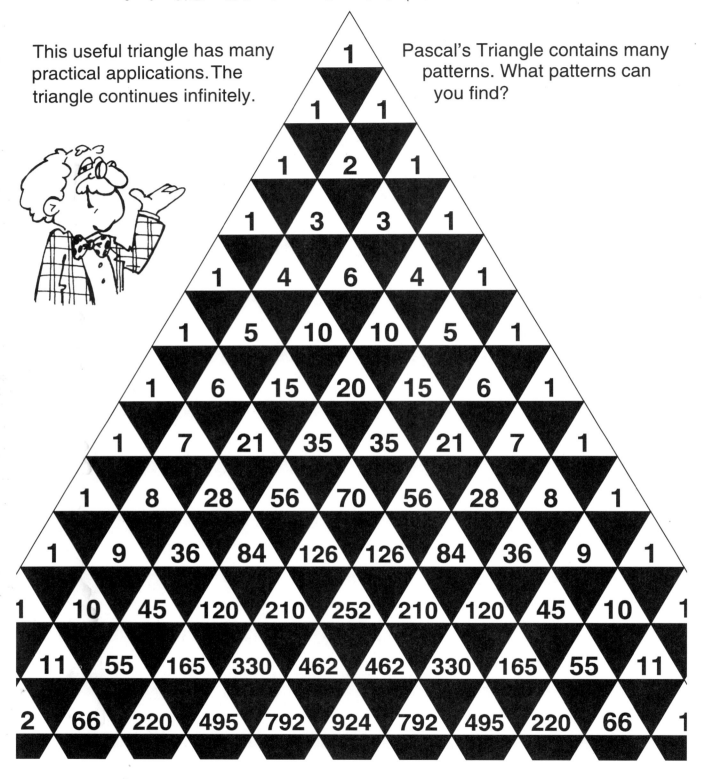

Triangular Numbers in Pascal's Triangle

Numbers arranged in a triangular array are called **triangular numbers**. Triangula numbers appear in Pascal's Triangle.

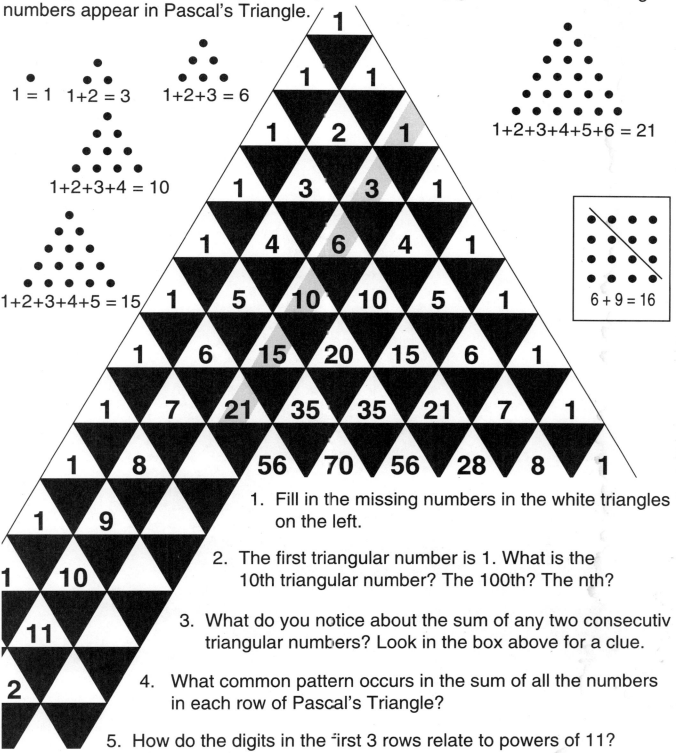

1 = 1   1+2 = 3   1+2+3 = 6

1+2+3+4 = 10

1+2+3+4+5 = 15

1+2+3+4+5+6 = 21

6 + 9 = 16

1. Fill in the missing numbers in the white triangles on the left.

2. The first triangular number is 1. What is the 10th triangular number? The 100th? The nth?

3. What do you notice about the sum of any two consecutiv triangular numbers? Look in the box above for a clue.

4. What common pattern occurs in the sum of all the numbers in each row of Pascal's Triangle?

5. How do the digits in the first 3 rows relate to powers of 11? Does the pattern continue down the triangle?

ODD AND EVEN NUMBERS IN PASCAL'S TRIANGLE

HISTORIC PROBLEM

A story is told about the famous mathematician, Carl Friedrich Gauss. When he was ten years old, his teacher presented the class with the following problem. "Find the sum of the first 100 counting numbers." While Carl's classmates were adding numbers on their slates, he just thought about the problem.

Using the approach Carl used:

1. Find the sum of the first 1000 counting numbers. _____

2. Find the sum of the first 333 counting numbers. _____

3. Find the sum of 37 + 38 + 39 + . . . + 90 + 91 + 92. _____

4. What is the sum of the first 100 odd numbers? _____

5. Find the sum of the first n counting numbers. _____

6. What is the next-to-last number in the first n counting numbers? _____

HOW MANY SQUARES?

Problem: How many different squares are in the figure at the right?

_____ squares

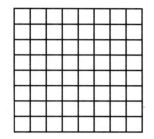 

The problem above is a tough one because there are squares of many sizes.
Searching for patterns is a very helpful technique in problems like this.
Let's see how Margo approached the problem.

If figure had been...	Small sqs	2x2 sqs	3x3 sqs	4x4 sqs	5x5 sqs	Pattern	Ans.
□	□ 1					1	**1**
(2x2 figure)	□ 4	□ 1				1+4	**5**
(3x3 figure)	□ 9	□ 4	□ 1			1+4+9	**14**
(4x4 figure)	□ 16	□ 9	□ 4	□ 1		1+4+9+16	**30**
(5x5 figure)	□ 25	□ 16	□ 9	□ 4	□ 1	1+4+9+16+25	**55**
6 x 6	___	___	___	___	___	___	___
7 x 7	___	___	___	___	___	___	___
8 x 8	___	___	___	___	___	___	___
10 x 10	___	___	___	___	___	___	___
n x n	___	___	___	___	___	___	___

Study the chart. Find the patterns and fill in the blanks.

Transition

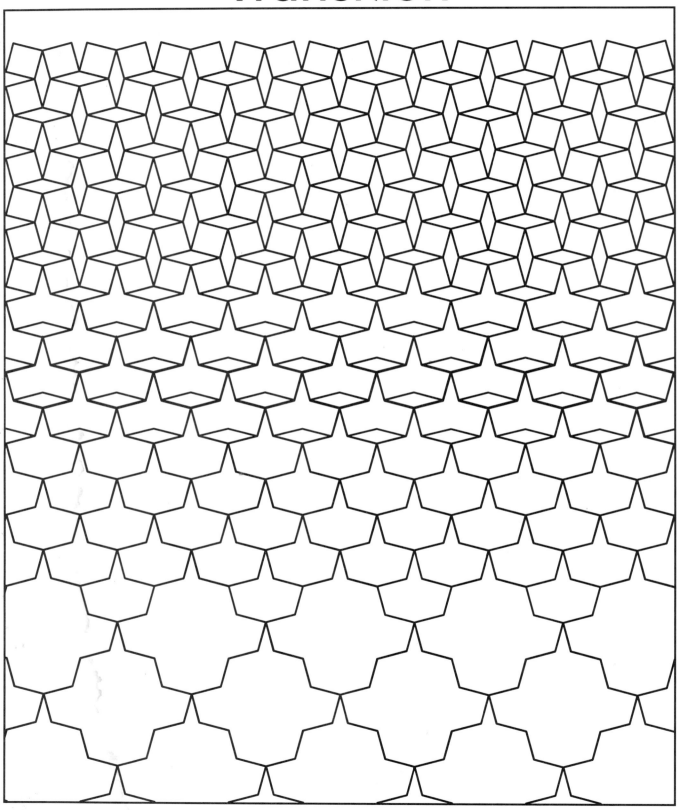

DIAMOND DILEMMA

Nine men—Brown, Jung, Adams, Lopez, Green, Hamada, Knight, Moreno, and Cohen—play on a baseball team. From the following information, determine the position played by each man.

- Brown and Moreno went to a movie with the pitcher.

- Hamada is taller than Knight and shorter than Jung, but each weighs more than the first baseman.

- The third baseman lives in the same apartment house as Cohen.

- Lopez and the outfielders go fishing in their spare time.

- Jung, Lopez, Brown, the right fielder, and the center fielder are the only men who have never been married.

- Of Adams and Knight, one plays the outfield.

- The right fielder is shorter than the center fielder.

- The third baseman is a brother of the pitcher's wife.

- Green is taller than the infielders and the battery (pitcher & catcher), except for Cohen, Moreno and Adams.

- The second baseman beat Cohen, Brown, Hamada, and the catcher at cards.

	catcher	pitcher	1st base	2nd base	shortstop	3rd base	right field	center field	left field
Brown									
Jung									
Adams									
Lopez									
Green									
Hamada									
Knight									
Moreno									
Cohen									

- The third baseman, the shortstop, and Hamada like country music.

- The second baseman is engaged to Lopez's sister.

- Adams lives in the same house as his sister but dislikes the catcher.

- Adams, Brown, and the shortstop have new cars.

- The catcher has three daughters, the third baseman has two sons, but Green is being sued for divorce.

SLIDES, FLIPS, AND TURNS

Observe the examples of slides, flips, and turns. Then, in each problem, sketch the design as slid, flipped, or turned as indicated.

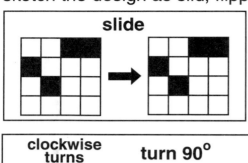 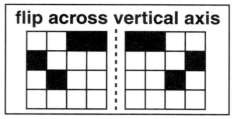 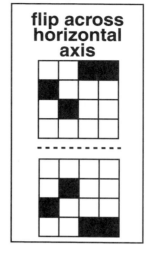

slide | flip across vertical axis | flip across horizontal axis

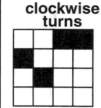   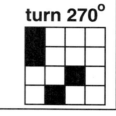

clockwise turns | turn 90° | turn 180° | turn 270°

1.    a. Slide   b. Flip step a. across vertical axis   c. Turn step b. 90°

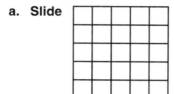 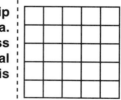 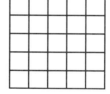

2. 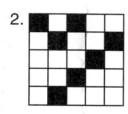   a. Flip across horizontal axis   b. Turn step a. 90°   c. Flip step b. across vertical axis

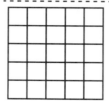 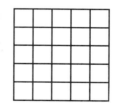 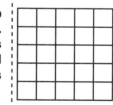

3. 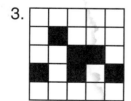   a. Turn 180°   b. Turn step a. 90°   c. Flip step b. across vertical axis

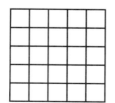 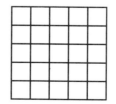

4. 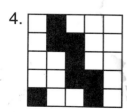   a. Turn 270°   b. Flip step a. across horizontal axis   c. Turn step b. 90° counter-clockwise

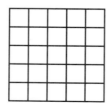 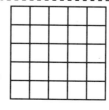 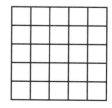

PROBLEM SOLVING
Mathematics is the study of patterns

Observe patterns to solve the problems on this page.

1. An interesting pattern concerning the one's digit in powers of thirteen is shown below.

   $1^{13} = 1$ $6^{13} = \ldots 6$ $11^{13} = \ldots 1$

   $2^{13} = \ldots 2$ $7^{13} = \ldots 7$ $12^{13} = \ldots 2$

   $3^{13} = \ldots 3$ $8^{13} = \ldots 8$ $13^{13} = \ldots 3$

   $4^{13} = \ldots 4$ $9^{13} = \ldots 9$ $14^{13} = \ldots 4$

   $5^{13} = \ldots 5$ $10^{13} = \ldots 10$

   a. What is the last digit in 2^{13}? _____

   b. What is the last digit in n^{13}? _____

   c. What is the last digit in $(5^{13})^{13}$? _____

2. One is correct. Which one? _____

   a. $2^{26} = 67,108,864$

   b. $2^{26} = 67,108,865$

   c. $2^{26} = 67,108,862$

3. Can 1000 be written as the sum of consecutive numbers? _____
   If so, give a solution. If not, explain why it can't.

NUMBER NAMES

Power	Number Name	Latin Root	Numerical Equivalent of Root
10^9	Billion	Bi	2
10^{12}	Trillion	Tri	3
10^{15}	Quadrillion	Quater	4
10^{18}	Quintillion	Quintus	5
10^{21}	Sextillion	Sex	6
10^{24}	Septillion	Septem	7
10^{27}	Octillion	Octo	8
10^{30}	Nonillion	Novem	9
10^{33}	Decillion	Decem	10
10^{36}	Undecillion	Undecim	11
10^{39}	Duodecillion	Duodecim	12
10^{42}	Tredecillion	Tredecim	13
10^{45}	Quattourdecillion	Quattordecim	14
10^{48}	Quindecillion	Quindecim	15
10^{51}	Sexdecillion	Sexdecim	16
10^{54}	Septendecillion	Septendecim	17
10^{57}	Ocodecillion	Octodecim	18
10^{60}	Novemdecillion	Novemdecim	19
10^{63}	Vigintillion	Viginti	20
10^{100}	Googol *	------------------	---

* Name invented by a 10-year-old American boy

Resources

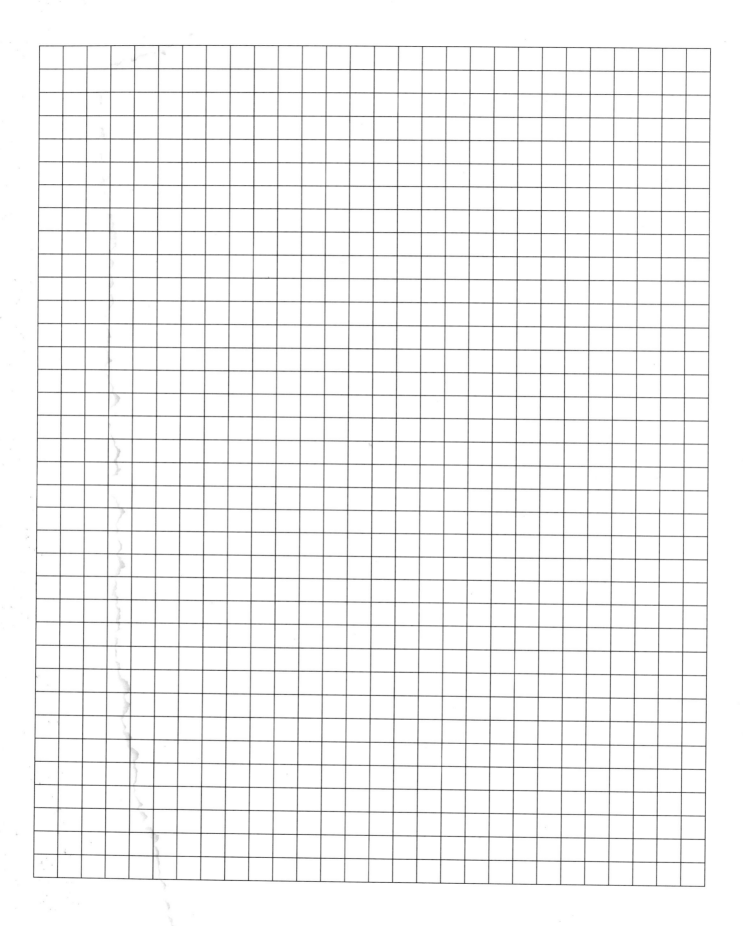

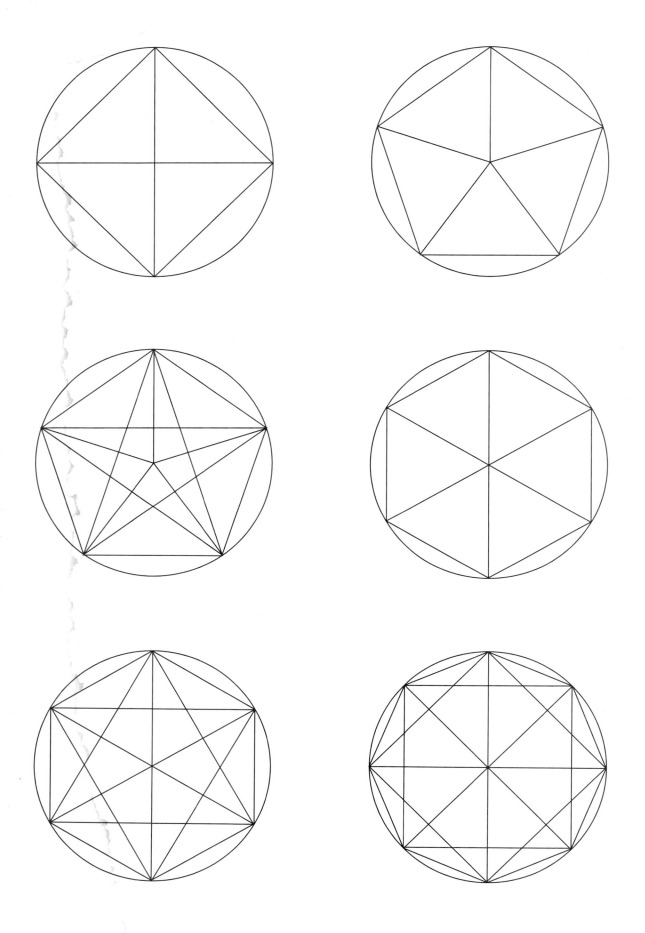

Smart Answers

1 How Many?
1. 20
2. 13
3. 7
4. 9
5. 8
6. 36

2 Is This Hat Taller. . .?
No. Its brim width is the same as its height.

3 Number Puzzle

	7	6	4	3			
	4	1	2	1	0	8	
3	0	6	0	0	7	0	1
5	5	4			2	8	3
6	4	0			8	5	0
7	1	0	3	5	0	9	6
	9	2	0	0	0	7	
		9	9	2	8		

4 Sum Strings
For instance, the digits 9-9-3-1 could be used to create the numbers 1399, 1939, 1993, 3199, 3919, 3991, 9139, 9193, 9319, 9391, 9913, and 9931. As the problem is stated, only one of these can be used. Other combinations of four digits that total 22 are: 9-9-2-2, 9-8-4-1, 9-8-3-2, 9-7-5-1, 9-7-4-2, 9-7-3-3, 9-6-6-1, 9-6-5-2, 9-6-4-3, 9-5-5-3, 9-5-4-4, 8-8-5-1, 8-8-4-2, 8-8-3-3, 8-7-6-1, 8-7-5-2, 8-7-4-3, 8-6-6-2, 8-6-5-3, 8-6-4-4, 8-5-5-4, 7-7-7-1, 7-7-6-2, 7-7-5-3, 7-7-4-4, 7-6-6-3, 7-6-5-4, 7-5-5-5, 6-6-6-4, and 6-6-5-5.

5 Symmetry

7 Juggling Digits

1. An organized list of all three-digit numbers whose digit sum is 5.

104	131	212	302	401
113	140	221	311	410
122	203	230	320	500

2. Make an organized list of all three-digit numbers whose digit sum is 6.

105	150	240	402	600
114	204	303	411	
123	213	312	420	
132	222	321	501	
141	231	330	510	

3. Make an organized list of all three-digit odd numbers whose digit sum is 9.

117	207	315	423	603
135	225	333	441	621
153	243	351	513	711
171	261	405	531	801

8 Drawing Patterns

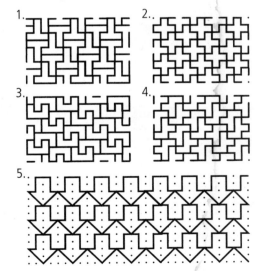

1 How Many?

1. 20

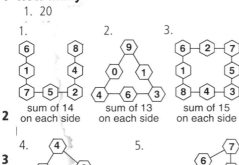

1. sum of 14 on each side	2. sum of 13 on each side	3. sum of 15 on each side

2

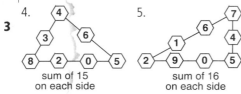

3

4. sum of 15 on each side	5. sum of 16 on each side

4 Sum Strings

For instance, the digits 9-9-3-1 could be used to create the numbers 1399, 1939, 1993, 3199, 3919, 3991, 9139, 9193, 9319, 9391, 9913, and 9931. As the problem is stated, only one of these can be used. Other combinations of four digits that total 22 are: 9-9-2-2, 9-8-4-1, 9-8-3-2, 9-7-5-1, 9-7-4-2, 9-7-3-3, 9-6-6-1, 9-6-5-2, 9-6-4-3, 9-5-5-3, 9-5-4-4, 8-8-5-1, 8-8-4-2, 8-8-3-3, 8-7-6-1, 8-7-5-2, 8-7-4-3, 8-6-6-2, 8-6-5-3, 8-6-4-4, 8-5-5-4, 7-7-7-1, 7-7-6-2, 7-7-5-3, 7-7-4-4, 7-6-6-3, 7-6-5-4, 7-5-5-5, 6-6-6-4, and 6-6-5-5.

5 Symmetry

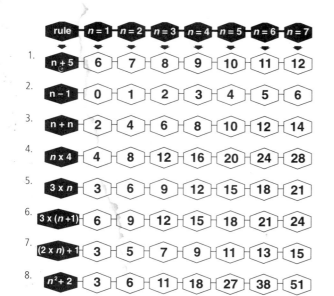

7 Juggling Digits

1. An organized list of all three-digit numbers whose digit sum is 5.

2. Make an organized list of all three-digit numbers whose digit sum is 6.

1.

2	3	8
9	1	4
7	5	6

2.

6	1	4
2	8	5
7	3	9

...zed list of all three-digit odd numbers ...is 9.

8 |

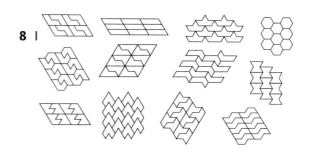

25 Relationships
1. B is five times A.
2. A is greater than C.
3. C is greater than A.
4. A is divisible by B.
5. C is greater than A.
6. B is 3/2 of A.
7. B is the square of A.
8. B is greater than A.
9. C is greater than A (or 9/2 of A).

27 Box Unfolding
1. c
2. a
3. d
4. a

28 Drawing Patterns

29 Problems to Solve
1. With three cuts, cut lengths of 32, 16, 8 and 4 links. With each of the cut links counted as 1 link, you can make any number from 1 to 63.
2. 6th is 21; 7th is 28; 10th is 55; the 100th is 5050.
3.
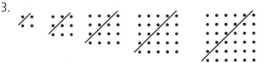

31 Helpful Crossouts
Race 2: Order of finish was D B A E C.
Race 9: Order of finish was A D F B C E.

32 Same Shapes
2 & 18, 8 & 27, 14 & 26, 20 & 29, 22 & 25

33 Factor Bingo
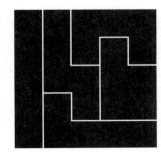

	Perfect Score	
3 in a row: $\boxed{3}$ × 3 =		9
4 in a row: $\boxed{1}$ × 4 =		4
5 in a row: $\boxed{2}$ × 5 =		10
Total Score		$\boxed{23}$

35 Helpful Crossouts
Race 4:Order of finish was C E B A F D.
Race 7:Order of finish was 5 1 3 2 6 4.

36 Being Observant
Answers may vary.
1. Powers of 2
2. Equilateral polygons
3. Regular polygons
4. Powers of 11
5. One more than a square number
6. Isosceles triangles

37 Target Practice
Answers will vary.
1. $5 \times 1 + 3 = 8$
2. $4 \times 2 + 5 = 13$
3. $4 \times 2 - 5 = 3$
4. $6 \times 3 + 5 = 23$
5. $5 \times 2 + 1 = 11$
6. $5 \times 4 - 2 = 18$
7. $2 \times 5 - 4 = 6$
8. $6 \times 3 - 9 = 9$

39 Wheel of Fraction
Treasure

40 Polyomino Puzzle

41 Puzzle Pieces
1. d
2. 1. f 2. i
   3. b 4. c
   5. j 6. e
   7. h 8. d
   9. g 10. a
3. a

43 Matchstick Puzzles

1.

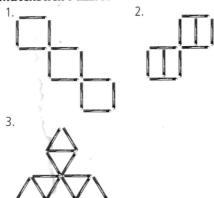

2.

3.

44 Polyominoes

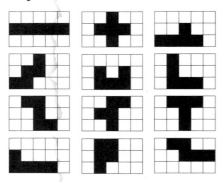

45 Ring Things

1.

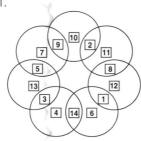

2. Ring 2

47 Winning Ways

1. Win in 5 games:
WWWLW

Win in 6 games:
WLWWLW   WWLWLW   WWLLWW
WWWLLW

Win in 7 games:
LLLWWWW	LLWLWWW	LLWWLWW
LLWWWLW	LWLLWWW	LWLWLWW
LWLWWLW	LWWLLWW	LWWWLWW
LWWWWLL	WLLLWWW	WLLWLWW
WLLWWLW	WLWLLWW	WLWLWLW
WLWWLLW	WWLLLWW	WWLLWLW
WWLWLLW	WWWLLLW	

2. There are 35 ways either team can win the World Series. So, altogether, there are 70 possibilities. One of those is that the National League will win in four games. Therefore, the probability (or chance) of that event is 1 out of 70.

3. 8 out of 70, or $\frac{4}{35}$.

4. 10 out of 70, or $\frac{1}{7}$.

5. 40 out of 70, or $\frac{4}{7}$.

6. 30 out of 70, or $\frac{3}{7}$.

7. Answers will vary but may include advertisers, TV stations, and local merchants.

53 Box Folding

1. b
2. b
3. a
4. a

54 Square Puzzle

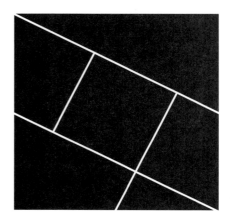

55 Who Am I?

1. 23
2. 44
3. 816
4. 49

57 Sum Shapes

1. Make a sum shape of 14 on each side.

2. Make a sum shape of 15 on each side.

3. Make a sum shape of 16 on each side.

4. Make a sum shape of 17 on each side.

58 Same Shapes
    1. o & v; b & n; e & s   2. e & y; b & x; h & v

59 Grouping Numbers
    1. $(5 + 3) \times 4 = 32$ 2. $5 + (3 \times 4) = 17$
    3. $(12 \div 4) - 2 = 1$ 4. $12 \div (4 - 2) = 6$
    5. $(15 - 5) - 2 = 8$ 6. $15 - (5 - 2) = 12$
    7. $(3 \times 8) (2 = 22$ 8. $3 \times (8 - 2) = 18$
    9. $3 \times (6 + 1) = 21$ 10. $(3 \times 6) + 1 = 19$
    11. $(12 \div 2) \times 2 = 12$ 12. $12 \div (2 \times 2) = 3$

61 How Many?
    1. 6   2. 21   3. 8
    4. 5   5. 6   6. 7

62 What Fractional Part?
    1. $\frac{1}{2}$ 2. $\frac{1}{2}$ 3. $\frac{1}{2}$ 4. $\frac{1}{4}$
    5. $\frac{1}{2}$ 6. $\frac{3}{8}$ 7. $\frac{5}{8}$ 8. $\frac{3}{8}$
    9. $\frac{5}{8}$ 10. $\frac{3}{8}$ 11. $\frac{5}{8}$ 12. $\frac{7}{16}$
    13. $\frac{13}{32}$ 14. $\frac{3}{16}$

63 Alpha-Numeric Puzzles
Answers may vary.

1.
```
   E          4
   Z          8
 +AS        +92
 ----      -----
 PIE        104
```
2.
```
 ONE        342
 ONE        342
+ONE       +342
-----      -----
TREY       1026
```
3.
```
  OO         33
  SA         74
 CAN        640
 + U        + 8
 ----      -----
 SEE        755
```
4.
```
 WIN        820
+THE       +675
-----      -----
GAME       1495
```

65 Drawing Angles
Line passes through:
    1. f'   2. u   3. p   4. b'
    5. q'   6. o'   7. q'   8. l

69 Visual Thinking
    1. a. 5   b. 3   c. 6   d. 2
       e. 2   f. 0   g. 1   h. infinite number
    2. a. green   b. yellow
    3. Answers will vary but may include:

70 The H Puzzle

71 Digit Dilemmas
    1. 986
    2. 121
    3. 225
    4. 864

72 Letter Symmetry
    1. 2, 5, 8, 14, 17, 18, 19, 20, 21, 24, 25, 27, 28
    2. 3, 7, 13, 28, 20, 21, 22, 24, 26
       Note: Several other E's are very close to being horizontally symmetric, but the lower part of the letter is slightly larger than the upper part.
    3. a, t, u, w, x, z
       Note: Several other H's are very close to being horizontally symmetric, but the lower part of the letter is slightly larger than the upper part.

73 Box Unfolding
    1. c
    2. d
    3. c
    4. b

75 Problems To Solve
    1. 1, 2, 4, 5, 7, 10, 13
       (As soon as three numbers in a row are possible, all ensuing numbers are possible, because three can be added to each.)
    2. 83
    3. Answers will vary.
       $30 = 7 + 23$
       $32 = 3 + 29$
       $34 = 3 + 31$
       $36 = 5 + 31$
       $38 = 7 + 31$
       $40 = 3 + 37$
       $42 = 5 + 37$
       $44 = 3 + 41$
       $46 = 5 + 41$
       $48 = 7 + 41$
       $50 = 3 + 47$
       $52 = 5 + 47$
       $54 = 7 + 47$
       $56 = 13 + 43$

77 Straight Eight

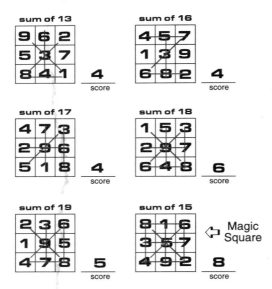

These are our "expert" scores. Rotation of solution (i.e., order of digits) may vary. If you beat these "experts," write and tell us your solutions.

79 What Direction?
1. SE
2. NW
3. E
4. W
5. SE
6. N
7. NE
8. NW
9. a
10. a
11. 2200 miles
12. 2000 miles
13. 2600 miles
14. 2600 miles

81 Alpha-Numeric Puzzles
Answers will vary.

1.

```
WHAT   5 2 4 8
+ NOS  +3 6 9
WORK   5 6 1 7
```

2.

```
A D D   1 3 3
M E        7 0
+ U P   + 5 4
S U M   2 5 7
```

3.

```
  ONE    5 6 0
+MORE   3 5 7 0
 TIME   4 1 3 0
```

4.

```
NOT    9 5 2
+ SO   +  8 5
EAZY   1 0 3 7
```

83 Target Practice
1. $8 + (7 \div 7) = 9$
2. $(15 - 9) + 3 = 9$
3. $(11 - 5) + 3 = 9$
4. $17 + (9 \div 9) = 18$
5. $(13 - 7) + 1 = 7$
6. $(8 - 2) \div 3 = 2$
7. $(15 - 9) - 3 = 3$
8. $(6 + 4) - 9 = 1$

84 Eight Congruent Squares
Some of the possible designs:

85 Fraction Size

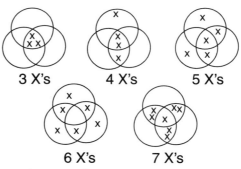

87 License To Count
1. $26^2 \times 10^4$, or 6,760,000
2. $26^2 \times 10^5$, or 67,600,000
3. $3 \times 26^3 \times 10^3$, or 52,728,000

89 Visual Thinking
1. e and i
2. Answers may vary but may include:

3 X's 4 X's 5 X's

6 X's 7 X's

3. The pattern for Box B:

90 Pascal's Triangle

Here are a few patterns:

Any number in the triangle is the sum of the two numbers directly above.

The sum of all of the numbers in any row is a power of two.

The counting numbers are in a diagonal.

The triangular numbers are in a diagonal.

The triangle is vertically symmetric.

The sum of all of the numbers above a given row is always one less than a power of two (e.g., 1, 3, 7, 15, 31).

Each entire row is a power of 11 (e.g., $1 = 11^0$, $11 = 11^1$, $121 = 11^2$, $1331 = 11^3$).

91 Triangular Numbers in Pascal's Triangle

1. 28, 36, 45, 55, 66, 78
2. 10th is 55. 100th is 5050. nth is $\frac{n(n + 1)}{2}$.
3. The sum of any two consecutive triangular numbers is a square number.
4. The sum of the numbers in any row is a power of two.
5. $1 = 11^0$, $11 = 11^1$, $121 = 11^2$, $1331 = 11^3$.

   Yes, the pattern continues. To illustrate the pattern, any number containing two or more digits must be "regrouped" according to the place-value positions of its digits. For instance, in the sixth row, the third triangle from the right is 10; as the third place-value represents 100s, the equivalent value here would be 10 X 100, or 1000. So, place 0 in the third digit position and carry the 1 to the fourth column. Add this to the value in that fourth triangle (10), forming 11 in the fourth column. Leave the 1 in that column, and carry the tens-place value of 10 to the next, fifth triangle. That triangle value is 5; adding the 1 from the 10 value yields a digit of 6 for this column. The leftmost triangle is 1. So, the final value for the sixth row is 161,051, which equals 11^5.

93 Historic Problem

1. 500,500
2. 55,611
3. 3612
4. 10,000
5. $\frac{n(n+ 1)}{2}$
6. $n - 1$

95 How Many Squares?

1. 204 squares altogether
2.

$n \times n$	n	$(n - 1)^2$	$(n - 2)^2$	$(n - 3)^2$	$(n - 4)^2$	$1 + 4 + \ldots + n^2$	
6×6	36	25	16	9	4	$1 + 4 + \ldots + 36$	91
7×7	49	36	25	16	9	$1 + 4 + \ldots + 49$	140
8×8	64	49	36	25	16	$1 + 4 + \ldots + 64$	204
9×9	81	64	49	36	25	$1 + 4 + \ldots + 81$	285
10×10	100	81	64	49	36	$1 + 4 + \ldots + 100$	385

97 Diamond Dilemma

	catcher	pitcher	1st base	2nd base	shortstop	3rd base	right field	center field	left field
Brown	X	X	O	X	X	X	X	X	X
Jung	X	X	X	O	X	X	X	X	X
Adams	X	X	X	X	O	X	X	X	X
Lopez	X	X	X	O	X	X	X	X	X
Green	X	X	X	X	X	X	X	X	O
Hamada	X	X	X	X	X	X	X	O	X
Knight	X	X	X	X	X	O	X	X	X
Moreno	O	X	X	X	X	X	X	X	X
Cohen	X	O	X	X	X	X	X	X	X

98 Slides, Flips and Turns

99 Problem Solving

1. a. 2
   b. Units digit of n.
   c. 5
2. a
3. Yes.   198 + 199 + 200 + 201 + 202 = 1000

More Smart Books

Locate the puzzle, activity, or challenge that interests you. Then match the corresponding numbers in "Smart Books to Check" with the numbered books on the facing page.

Page	Puzzles, Challenges, and Activities	Smart Books to Check (see page 119)
1	How Many?	38, 48
2	Is This Hat Taller?	5, 51
4	Sum Strings	44, 46
5	Symmetry	22, 26
6	Visual: Rotating Hexagons	41, 43
8	Drawing Patterns	42
9	Sum Shapes	34, 44
10	Regular Polygons	39
12	Which One Differs?	36, 48
13	Straight-Line Curves	41, 43
14	Visual: Checkered Hexagons	17
17	Target Practice	46
18	Visual: Rotating Circles	41, 43
19	Tic-Tac-Number	8, 49
20	Polly's Print Patterns	16, 42
21	Visual Thinking	26, 48
22	Geometric Patterns	41, 43
23	Common Cents or Common Sense?	34, 38
24	Symmetry in Design	48
26	Visual: Inscribed Pentagons	41, 43
27	Box Unfolding	36, 48
28	Drawing Patterns	42, 48
29	Problems to Solve	34, 38
30	Impossible Arrangement	5, 13
31	Helpful Crossouts	49, 54
32	Same Shapes	10, 22
33	Factor Bingo	34
34	Two Horizontal Lines	5, 51
35	Helpful Crossouts	49, 54

Page	Puzzles, Challenges, and Activities	Smart Books to Check (see page 119)
36	Being Observant	3, 34
37	Target Practice	46
38	Visual: Five-pointed Stars	33, 39
39	Wheel of Fraction	48
40	Polyomino Puzzle	11, 16
41	Puzzle Pieces	42, 48
42	Photo: Roofs	28, 53
43	Matchstick Puzzles	7
44	Polyominoes	11, 16
45	Ring Things	36, 48
46	Geometric Patterns in Quilts	9, 42
47	Winning Ways	38, 49
48	Basic Geometric Constructions	35, 39
49	Can You Construct These?	35, 39
50	Visual: Star Designs	35, 39
51	Creating a Design	35, 39
52	Constructing a Regular Pentagon	35, 39
53	Box Folding	26, 48
54	Square Puzzle	23
55	Who Am I?	40
57	Sum Shapes	44
58	Same Shapes	48
59	Grouping Numbers	46
60	Visual: Star Designs	35, 39
61	How Many?	38, 48
62	What Fractional Part?	10, 36
63	Alpha-Numeric Puzzles	6
64	Visual: Rings of Squares	2, 66
66	Visual: Kaleidoscope Designs	14

Page	Puzzles, Challenges, and Activities	Smart Books to Check (see page 119)
67	Kaleidoscope Design	14
69	Visual Thinking	36, 48
70	The H Puzzle	23
71	Digit Dilemmas	3, 37
72	Symmetry in Letters	48
73	Box Unfolding	26, 48
74	Visual: Optical Illusion	5, 51
75	Problems to Solve	34, 37
76	Tessellating	42
77	Straight Eight	44
80	Geometric Patterns	42
81	Alpha-Numeric Puzzles	6
82	Visual: Inscribed Hexagons	41, 43
83	Target Practice	46
84	Eight Congruent Squares	5, 51
87	License to Count	37
88	Geometric Patterns	42
89	Visual Thinking	36, 48
90	Pascal's Triangle	18, 47
91	Triangular Numbers in Pascal's Triangle	18, 47
92	Odd and Even Numbers in Pascal's Triangle	18, 47
93	Historic Problem	38
94	Visual: Deltoids	41, 43
95	How Many Squares?	38
96	Transition	42
97	Diamond Dilemma	49, 54
98	Slides, Flips, and Turns	22
99	Problem Solving	3, 37
100	Number Names	37

1. Agostini, Franco. *Math and Logic Games*. New York: Harper and Row, 1983.
2. Beard, Col. Robert S. *Patterns In Space*. Chicago: Creative Publications, 1973.
3. Bezuska, Stanley, and Margaret Kenney. *Number Treasury*. Parsippany, NJ: Dale Seymour Publications, 1982.
4. Blackwell, William. *Geometry in Architecture*. Berkeley, CA: Key Curriculum Press, 1984.
5. Block, J. R., and H. E. Yuker. *Can You Believe Your Eyes?* New York: Gardner Press, 1989.
6. Brooke, Maxey. *150 Puzzles in Crypt-Arithmetic*. New York: Dover Publications, 1969.
7. Brooke, Maxey. Tricks, *Games and Puzzles With Matches*. New York: Dover Publications, 1973.
8. Clark, Dave. *More Tic-Tac-Toe Math*. Parsippany, NJ: Dale Seymour Publications, 1996.
9. Cohen, Luanne Seymour. *Quilt Design Masters*. Parsippany, NJ: Dale Seymour Publications, 1996.
10. Davidson, Patricia, and Robert Willcut. *Spatial Problem Solving*. Parsippany, NJ: Cuisenaire Co. of America, 1984.
11. Duby, Marjorie. *Try It! Pentaminoes*. Parsippany, NJ: Cuisenaire Co. of America, 1992.
12. El-Said, Issam, and Ayse Parman. *Geometric Concepts in Islamic Art*. Parsippany, NJ: Dale Seymour Publications, 1976.
13. Ernst, Bruno. *Adventures With Impossible Figures*. Norfolk, England: Tarquin Publications, 1987.
14. Finkel, Norma Yvette, and Leslie Finkel. *Kaleidoscope Designs and How to Create Them*. New York: Dover Publications, 1980.
15. Fisher, Lyle. *Super Problems*. Parsippany, NJ: Dale Seymour Publications, 1982.
16. Golomb, Solomon. *Polyominoes,* Rev. Ed. Princeton, NJ: Princeton University Press, 1994.
17. Grafton, Carol Belanger. *Optical Designs in Motion With Moiré Overlays*. New York: Dover Publications, 1976.
18. Green, Thomas, and Charles Hamburg. *Pascal's Triangle*. Parsippany, NJ: Dale Seymour Publications, 1986.
19. Kennedy, Joe, and Diane Thomas. *Kaleidoscope Math*. Chicago; Creative Publications, 1978.
20. Kenneway, Eric. *Complete Origami*. New York: St Martin's Press, 1987.
21. Kremer, Ron. *Exploring With Squares and Cubes*. Parsippany, NJ: Dale Seymour Publications, 1989.
22. Kroner, Louis R. *Slides, Flips and Turns*. Parsippany, NJ: Dale Seymour Publications, 1984.
23. Lindgren, Harry. *Recreational Problems In Geometric Dissections*. New York: Dover Publications, 1972.
24. McKim, Robert. *Thinking Visually*. Parsippany, NJ: Dale Seymour Publications, 1997.
25. Moran, Jim. *The Wonders of Magic Squares*. New York: Vintage Books, 1982.
26. Murray, William, and Francis Rigney. *Paper Folding For Beginners*. New York: Dover Publications, 1960.
27. Neale, Robert, and Thomas Hull. *Origami, Plain and Simple*. New York: St Martin's Press, 1994.
28. Norwich, John Julius, ed., et al. *Great Architecture of the World*. New York: Da Capo Press, 1991.
29. Pearce, Peter, and Susan Pearce. *Polyhedra Primer*. Parsippany, NJ: Dale Seymour Publications, 1978.
30. Picciotto, Henri. *Pentamino Activities, Lessons and Puzzles*. Chicago: Creative Publications, 1986.
31. Pollard, Jeanne. *Building Toothpick Bridges*. Parsippany, NJ: Dale Seymour Publications, 1985.
32. Rozell, Paula. *Plotting Pictures;* Grades 5–8. Parsippany, NJ: Dale Seymour Publications, 1997.
33. Runion, Garth. *The Golden Section*. Parsippany, NJ: Dale Seymour Publications, 1990.
34. Seymour, Dale, Mary Laycock, Ruth Heller and Bob Larsen. *Aftermath* (Series). Chicago: Creative Publications, 1970.
35. Seymour, Dale, and Schadler Reuben. *Creative Constructions,* Rev. Ed. Chicago: Creative Publications, 1974.
36. Seymour, Dale, and Ed Beardslee. *Critical Thinking Activities* (Series). Parsippany, NJ: Dale Seymour Publications, 1988.
37. Seymour, Dale, and Richard Gidley. *Eureka,* Rev. Ed. Chicago: Creative Publications, 1972.
38. Seymour, Dale. *Favorite Problems*. Parsippany, NJ: Dale Seymour Publications, 1982.
39. Seymour, Dale. *Geometric Design*. Parsippany, NJ: Dale Seymour Publications, 1988.
40. Seymour, Dale, and John Gregory. *I'm a Number Game*. Chicago: Creative Publications, 1978.
41. Seymour, Dale. *Introduction to Line Designs*. Parsippany, NJ: Dale Seymour Publications, 1992.
42. Seymour, Dale, and Jill Britton. *Introduction to Tessellations*. Parsippany, NJ: Dale Seymour Publications, 1989.
43. Seymour, Dale, Linda Silvey and Joyce Snider. *Line Designs,* Rev. Ed. Chicago: Creative Publications, 1974.
44. Seymour, Dale. *Sum Puzzles*. Chicago: Creative Publications, 1979.
45. Seymour, Dale. *Tangramath*. Chicago: Creative Publications, 1971.
46. Seymour, Dale, and Margo Seymour. *Target Practice* (Series). Parsippany, NJ: Dale Seymour Publications, 1993.
47. Seymour, Dale. *Visual Patterns in Pascal's Triangle*. Parsippany, NJ: Dale Seymour Publications, 1986.
48. Seymour, Dale. *Visual Thinking Cards* (Series). Parsippany, NJ: Dale Seymour Publications, 1983.
49. Sherard, Wade H. III, *Logic Number Problems*. Parsippany, NJ: Dale Seymour Publications, 1997.
50. Silvey, Linda, and Loretta Taylor. *Paper and Scissors Polygons and More*. Parsippany, NJ: Dale Seymour Publications, 1997.
51. Simon, Seymour. *The Optical Illusions Book*. New York: Beech Tree Books, 1976.
52. Spangenburg, Ray, and Diane K. Moser. *The Story of American Bridges (Connecting a Continent Series)*. New York: Facts on File, 1991 (out of print).
53. Wilkinson, Philip, and Paolo Donati (illustrator). *Amazing Buildings*. London: DK Publishing, 1993.
54. Williams, Wayne. *Quizzles*. Parsippany, NJ: Dale Seymour Publications, 1997.

Smart Math Web Sites

In the time it takes to publish this book, a list of Web sites could easily become a bit out of date. With that caveat, here are sites that offer more mathematical puzzles, challenges, and beautiful images. If you find a site no longer available, try links from another site to newer sites on related topics. Explore!

Bullpup Math Resources. A middle-school site with toothpick (matchstick) puzzles, problem-of-the-day offerings, links to online math-problem contests, and links to online puzzle "rings" (strings of Web sites).
http://www.highland.madison.k12.il.us/jbasden

Enchanted Mind. Visual and logic puzzles, such as tangrams, pentominos, pyramids; variety from National Center for Creativity. Online and printable puzzles.
http://enchantedmind.com/puzzle.htm

Fibonacci and the Golden Section. Explanations, a page of easier Fibonacci puzzles, and applications in art, architecture, and music.
http://www.ee.surrey.ac.uk/Personal/R.Knott/Fibonacci/fib.html

Geometry Through Art.
http://forum.swarthmore.edu/~sarah/shapiro/

Interactive Mathematics Miscellany and Puzzles. Online and printable puzzles and games, fun even for those who "hate" math; also available on CD-ROM.
http://www.cut-the-knot.com/

Magic Squares. Unit for upper elementary and middle-school students.
http://forum.swarthmore.edu/alejandre/magic.square.html

Math Forum (Swarthmore College). Showcases great activities on specific math concepts, such as dividing by zero, magic squares, polyhedra, Pascal's triangle, making tessellations, famous math problems. Links to many math problems and puzzles on the Internet.
http://forum.swarthmore.edu/.

Mathematical Problem Solving Task Centres. Monthly mathematically-oriented problem for various grade levels, with past problems cataloged. From Mathematical Association of Victoria, Australia.
http://www.srl.rmit.edu.au/mav/PSTC/general/index.html

Pascal's Triangle. Lessons and worksheets.
http://forum.swarthmore.edu/workshops/usi/pascal/pascal_lessons.html#lessons

Perspective Drawing, Moebius Strip, Polyhedra, and Spreadsheets.
http://forum.swarthmore.edu/sum95/math_and/

Symbolic Sculpture and Mathematics. Gallery of mathematical sculptures by John Robinson (such as on page 86). Math explanations and construction tips on structures such as rings, bands, knots, and fractals.
http://www.bangor.ac.uk/SculMath/

Symmetry and Pattern: The Art of Oriental Carpets.
http://forum.swarthmore.edu/geometry/rugs/

Tessellation Tutorials. Tutorials teach students how to tessellate (somewhat in the style of M.C. Escher) using HyperCard or HyperStudio, ClarisWorks, LogoWriter, templates, or simple straightedge and compass.
http://forum.swarthmore.edu/sum95/suzanne/tess.intro.html

University of Minnesota Geometry Center Graphics Archive. Includes fractals, digital art, 3-D art, advanced topics such as tilings.
http://www.geom.umn.edu/graphics/

Virtual Polyhedra. Collection of over 1000 virtual-reality polyhedra to explore, with classroom ideas for making and exploring polyhedra.
http://www.li.net/~george/virtual-polyhedra/vp.html

World of Escher. Examples of Escher's work, background, and an annual tessellation contest for students, with winning images.
http://www.worldofescher.com/